# PREACHING
## FOR
# CHURCH
# TRANSFORMATION

## Other Books by Bill Easum

*Ministry in Hard Times*
with Bill Tenny-Brittian

*Winning on Purpose: How to Organize Congregations
to Succeed in Their Mission*
with Thomas G. Bandy and John Kaiser

*Sacred Cows Make Gourmet Burgers:
Ministry Anytime, Anywhere, by Anyone*

*A Second Resurrection: Leading Your Congregation to New Life*

*Go BIG with Small Groups:
Eleven Steps to an Explosive Small Group Ministry*
with John Atkinson

*Go BIG: Lead Your Church to Explosive Growth*
with Bil Cornelius

*The Complete Ministry Audit*

*Put on Your Own Oxygen Mask First: Rediscovering Ministry*

*The Nomadic Church:
Growing Your Congregation Without Owning the Building*
with Pete Theodore

*Unfreezing Moves: Following Jesus into the Mission Field*

# BILL EASUM

# PREACHING FOR CHURCH TRANSFORMATION

Abingdon Press
*Nashville*

# PREACHING FOR CHURCH TRANSFORMATION
*Copyright © 2010 by Bill Easum*

*This book is printed on acid-free paper.*

**Library of Congress Cataloging-in-Publication Data**

Easum, William M., 1939-
    Preaching for church transformation / Bill Easum.
        p.   cm.
    ISBN 978-1-4267-1062-9 (book- pbk./trade pbk., perfect binding : alk. paper)   1. Preaching.   2. Church growth.   3. Sermons, American.   4. United Methodist Church (U.S.)—Sermons.   I. Title.
    BV4221.E28 2010
    251'.02—dc22

                                                                        2010021124

All scripture quotations unless noted otherwise are taken from the New Revised Standard Version of the Bible, copyright 1989, Division of Christian Education of the National Council of the Churches of Christ in the United States of America. Used by permission. All rights reserved.

Scripture quotations marked "NKJV™" are taken from the New King James Version®. Copyright © 1982 by Thomas Nelson, Inc. Used by permission. All rights reserved.

Scripture quotations marked (NASB) are taken from the *New American Standard Bible*®, Copyright © 1960, 1962, 1963, 1968, 1971, 1972, 1973, 1975, 1977, 1995 by The Lockman Foundation. Used by permission. (www.Lockman.org)

Scripture quotations marked (NIV) are taken from the Holy Bible, NEW INTERNATIONAL VERSION®. Copyright © 1973, 1978, 1984 by International Bible Society. All rights reserved throughout the world. Used by permission of International Bible Society.

Scripture quotations marked (KJV) are taken from the King James or Authorized Version of the Bible.

Scripture quotations marked (NLT) are taken from the *Holy Bible,* New Living Translation, copyright © 1996. Used by permission of Tyndale House Publishers, Inc., Wheaton, Illinois 60189. All rights reserved.

10 11 12 13 14 15 16 17 18 19—10 9 8 7 6 5 4 3 2 1
MANUFACTURED IN THE UNITED STATES OF AMERICA

# ACKNOWLEDGMENTS

It's been my practice over the last few years to invite some friends into the writing of my books. I've found they always make them better books. I'm indebted to them for taking the time to be part of this journey.

Bruce Cole
Larry Glover-Wetherington
Jim Oates
Michael Deutsch
Matthew Woodcock
John Randall
Jan Blankenship
Greg Watling

# CONTENTS

Foreword: A Word from a Good Friend . . . . . . . . . . . . . . . . . . . . . . . . ix

How to Use This Book . . . . . . . . . . . . . . . . . . . . . . . . . . . . . . . . . . . xi

1. An Impossible Mission . . . . . . . . . . . . . . . . . . . . . . . . . . . . . . . 1

2. An Ever-widening Circle . . . . . . . . . . . . . . . . . . . . . . . . . . . . 19

3. The Two Imperatives of the Early Church
   and the Centrality of Jesus . . . . . . . . . . . . . . . . . . . . . . . . . . . 33

4. Looking Inward So We Can Turn Outward . . . . . . . . . . . . . . . . 43

5. Multiplying the Movement . . . . . . . . . . . . . . . . . . . . . . . . . . . 55

6. Sharing Your Story . . . . . . . . . . . . . . . . . . . . . . . . . . . . . . . . . 65

7. Backyard Missionaries . . . . . . . . . . . . . . . . . . . . . . . . . . . . . . 79

8. It's Not about You or Me; It's about the Kingdom . . . . . . . . . . . . 95

Afterword:
   Now That You've Read This Book and Before You Begin . . . . . 111

# Foreword

## A Word from a Good Friend

*A note to those who have already been in their churches for a while and are using Bill's book to turn the page to a new day:* if this book had been available to you as you began your ministry in the place where you are now leading, the conditions likely would have been different than they are now. For instance, your first six months in a new church are usually filled with amped-up energy, joy, excitement, and hope. If you've been able to sustain that kind of atmosphere past your first year, congratulations. More likely, if you are past your first year, the bloom is somewhat off the rose, and you are fully immersed in the hard work of daily leadership.

If the latter is the case, you may find yourself reading Bill's book and thinking, "Yes! This is exactly what I need to say to our people and exactly what they need to hear." You may be experiencing some of the frustration of leading a people who are stuck in a Sancho Panza world. If so, please heed this gentle warning: preaching the principles of this book as Bill lays them out will be experienced differently at this point in your ministry than if you had been coached to preach these principles beginning day one. You may be feeling frustrated at this point, where, at the beginning, you didn't yet have cause to be frustrated. Resistance will be higher among the Sancho Panzas of your church now that they are more used to your presence among them and more in tune to who you are—gifts and warts and all.

That doesn't mean you shouldn't follow the plan of Bill's book. Not at all. Better now than never. It does mean, however, that you will have to gut check and ask God to fill you with renewed joy and optimism. Without that joy, you may have only commitment and resolve. Those are key leadership traits always. But without joy, optimism, and—yes—love, your commitment and resolve will only be a "noisy gong and a clanging cymbal." You won't win many followers that way. Trust me—I learned this the hard way.

So before you launch into this series, ask God for a heart overflowing with joy. And when you have that joy, don't forget to tell your face.

– *A friend*

# HOW TO USE THIS BOOK

No matter where you're located, no matter what size your church, and no matter what situation in which you find yourself, what follows will lay an excellent foundation and be a workable teaching/preaching plan to move your church forward. You will want to tweak it to fit your personality and context, but embedding these basics into the fabric of your church will always serve you well.

I first shared a brief form of this series in my book *A Second Resurrection*. As a result, several readers suggested I elaborate on the content. So this book emerged a few years later.

The following chapters include the ideas and Scriptures I preached during my first eight months as the new pastor of a restart church I stayed at for twenty-four years and grew into one of the largest United Methodist churches in the country at the time (1969–93). The series also includes additional material I've collected over the years, as well as material from friends who have preached this material prior to its becoming a book and who have made suggestions about how to improve the messages.

I've written most of the book in preaching/teaching form rather than in print form. I have also used different versions of the Bible to fit my purpose. I encourage you to use whatever version you prefer.

Whether or not I was in my first few months as pastor, I would want to preach/teach from the following texts to lay the foundation for ministry. I share my thoughts on these texts with the knowledge that their lessons can be easily customized from church to church. You will find that most of the texts are chosen to get people to think outwardly rather than inwardly.

This book is not a commentary on the Acts of the Apostles. I made no effort to do a thorough exegesis of the entire book. The preaching suggestions in this book are geared toward transformation and are not a complete teaching on the Acts of the Apostles. I've intentionally selected only those texts that I feel can be used to move a church to and through transformation. Whether that transformation is for turnaround, restart, or going missional, these texts work. Surely, you will want to include some other passages not only from Acts but also from other parts of the Bible. But I do encourage you to use the texts I've included. They are the heart of Acts and the heart of a faithful church.

Get some good commentaries to help you formulate your message. But remember: it's not exegesis that's going to move your church forward; it's the passionate and consistent way you point your congregation toward its mission with Jesus.

At this moment in history, 80 to 90 percent of all established churches in North America are at risk. They are in need of resurrection, restart, turnaround, or going missional. I have chosen these texts to help you on your particular journey.

Keep in mind, you might find yourself spending several weeks on one chapter because it speaks profoundly to the needs of your congregation. Follow your own timeline.

I have included some personal stories just to give you the flavor of how I motivated a dead church to breathe again. You will need to supply your own stories or stories from your congregation.

Some of the sections will read as if I'm preaching to my church. Some sections will be directed more toward the ways you might preach the text in your particular situation. When that is the case, you will see the section highlighted like this example. These sections are helpful hints about how to proceed or where to look for further information or information about why I did what I did. Either way, you will see a passionate and direct way to preach to your people. My goal is for you to feel the passion of the text and be able to pass that passion on to your people.

I have included some key phrases in text boxes throughout the book in case you are using images and words on the screen while preaching. The same is true with all graphics included—feel free to use them in your church.

I have also included online several supporting articles and graphics that might aid you in presenting this series. To simplify matters, in the notes I will refer to this web page as the "support page." You can find the articles and graphics at http://churchconsultations.com/index.php?id=3064. They are free. If you are a member of The Community you can find a thousand images on our site, some of which will work for this series (once in The Community go to Community Resources, then to Graphics). If you're not a member, you can join by going here: http://churchconsultations.com/services/join-the-community/.

If you wish to learn more about coaching opportunities with me, go to http://churchconsultations.com/index.php?id=2868.

Have fun with the series and, at the same time, ask God to give you the passion to persuade, transform, and persist if and when the going gets rough.

# A N   I M P O S S I B L E   M I S S I O N

## K E Y   I D E A
WITH GOD ALL THINGS ARE POSSIBLE,
SO IT IS BEST TO DREAM THE IMPOSSIBLE.

You can't begin this series until you have a clear vision of where God wants your church to go, because somewhere in this message, you will need to share that vision with the congregation. If you don't have that vision, put this book down, take your Bible, and go off to a place where you can listen to God. Pray and ask God for a vision for the community he has called you to lead.

You may be thinking, "I can't know the vision until I've spent time with these people I'm leading." While it is true that your leadership vision will and should be shaped by those with whom you are following Jesus, the core of the vision must begin with you. God never gives a vision to a committee. God gives a vision to an individual, and it is the work of that individual to inspire and form people around that vision. Once you have a solid, vivid vision, continue with this book.

Remember, there could be several messages in this chapter. It depends on how depressed the church might be.

*Man of La Mancha* is one of my favorite musicals.[1] I'm captivated by two of its characters. Don Quixote is the dreamer of impossible dreams, lover of those who won't love him back, and tilter at windmills. The other character is Sancho Panza, the faithful follower who never dreamed of something better or dared to color outside the lines.

You may want to play the video of the actual scene where Don Quixote sings "The Impossible Dream" to the prostitute Aldonza, whom Quixote thinks is Dulcinea: http://www.youtube.com/watch?v=RfHnz YEHAow.

Sancho Panza reminds me of so many church people who are content with muddling along merely surviving. I don't know about you, but I don't want to pastor a church full of Sancho Panzas. I don't want to be part of a church that is content to merely survive. And I hope you don't either.

I want to be part of a church full of Don Quixotes who dream the impossible dream; who dare to take on the world and shake it till it rattles; who help people reach their God-given potential; who thrive on the inherent risks of the Great Commission and Great Commandment. And I'm trusting that you also want to be part of that kind of church.

## JOIN ME ON AN IMPOSSIBLE MISSION

My first Sunday morning, I asked the thirty-seven people present to join me on a journey to grow a church of thousands and transform the city of San Antonio. On the surface, it appeared to be an impossible mission. But we all know that nothing is impossible for God. They needed to hear that since they had failed to launch the church through two previous pastors. Whether your church is on its knees or poised to take off, this message has merits—you have to have a vision larger than life to lead a thriving church in today's environment.

You will have to fill in this message with the particulars of your situation. You will also have to make sure God has given you a mission large enough to capture the hearts and imaginations of key leaders in your church. If this is your first year as pastor of this church, you might want to read an article on that subject, because the last thing you want to do is pass up a golden opportunity to step out and lead. That opportunity won't come around again.[2] If your church is declining and you are attempting to turn it around, you would do well to read my article about the risks of turning around a church.[3]

If your church is in decline or on a plateau, during your opening message you may want to put a graph up that shows the seriousness of the situation. The worse it is, the more important to show the graphics. Remember: people change in direct proportion to their discontent level. So the higher their discontent, the better. Even if the church is on a plateau, the people in the pew are probably getting older every year. (The only exception is if the church is replacing its elderly members with younger ones.) So don't pull any punches. Paint them a picture of what is going to happen over the next few years. This preparation will be important to their response no matter what your situation, so don't ignore it.

Here's the graph I showed the church on my first Sunday morning. I put the graph up and then drew a line from 1963 down to 1969 and beyond, so the line went entirely off the graph. (I had to do this on an overhead projector. Aren't you glad you don't have to do that?) My only goal was to cause them to be discontent with the situation.

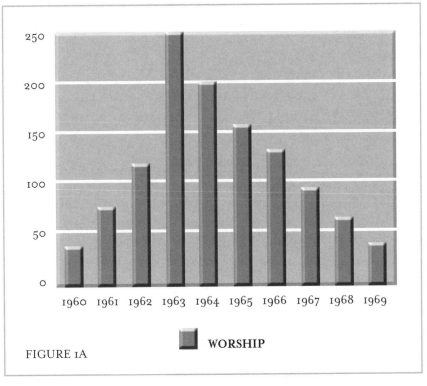

FIGURE 1A

WORSHIP

So, I'm asking you this morning to join me in what would appear to the normal eye to be an impossible journey. I'm asking you to join me in a mission to grow a church of thousands and to transform the city of San Antonio. You heard me correctly—to turn this small band of people into thousands of people whose actions will transform our city, our state, and our world.

We can do this. You know how I know? Because God tells us in the Scriptures we can. And the Apostle Paul tells us why. He reminds us that we "can do all things through [Christ] who strengthens [us]" (Phil. 4:13). Do we really believe these words? More importantly, how many of us live as if we believe it? All things are possible if we believe. Now, I know that is a big *if*. But I also know our God is a big God. The only thing that keeps God from achieving his dream for our world is us.

Begin now making a list of what your city might look like if transformation actually happened. List the things that need changing and how your church might take part in that change. Build this list as you go through this series, and be prepared to share some of your ideas when it seems appropriate in the series. In order to build this list, you will have to spend more time out in the city than you probably are spending at the moment. So set aside some time each week for this specific purpose. Later, you will be asked to form a small group of people to meet with each week. In time, you will want to involve them in compiling this list.

### Philippians 4:13

*"I can do all things through [Christ] who strengthens me."*

The first time I read this text, I stopped and asked myself, "Do I really believe this? If so, what do I have to change about my life?" All we have to do to answer that question is to watch Paul's incredible journey from being a Pharisee in Jerusalem to being the greatest Christian missionary of all time.

Paul was a great Christian missionary—the greatest of all time. It's been my observation that great Christians envision what seems to be an impossible goal, then push the envelope until they find their limits of possibility. I think that is what both Jesus and Paul are trying to tell us—that with God, it is possible for us to do whatever God asks us to do, even if it's to share our faith to the ends of the earth. I want to be a great Christian and trust you do also. It's time we stepped out on a mission with God.

This text poses a question we must answer during this series—if we really believe that all things are possible with God, what would we change about our lives and our church if we truly incorporate this text into our lives? We will spend some time in the next few months answering this question.

Now, how could Paul make such a statement? You have to remember that everything about Paul's life, even his name, was transformed when he met Christ. He didn't grow up in the church like many of us did. He didn't grow up knowing God's love. He grew up under the burden of religious legalism. But when he met Christ, all of that changed. As he said, "Therefore, if anyone is in Christ, he is a new creation; the old has gone, the new has come!" (2 Cor. 5:17 NIV).

## OUR ANCHOR: THE BOOK OF ACTS

Acts will be the anchor for my preaching for the next few months. I've chosen Acts because it chronicles the story of the birth and spread of the church throughout the known world. Without it we would have no knowledge of the early church, except what we could glean from Paul's writings.

Most authorities believe Luke, the physician, is the author of Acts. I do also. Therefore Acts could be considered the conclusion to the Gospel of Luke. If that is the case, then we know the reason Luke wrote Acts.

If you remember, in the last chapter of the Gospel of Luke Jesus is on the road to Emmaus with two travelers who do not recognize him until he eats dinner with them. The significance of traveling to Emmaus is that Emmaus was mostly a Roman garrison, a Gentile town. One of the last remembrances of Jesus in Luke's Gospel is of him traveling away from Jerusalem, away from the Temple, away from the Jewish world, away from the religious professionals, and toward the Gentile world.

That's like you and me walking away from the comfort of these four walls, away from rituals that are comfortable to us, away from our traditions, away from our man-made doctrines, into the world of the unchurched, dechurched, and never-churched world.

You see, the Gospel of Luke tells the story of the life of Jesus. Acts tells us about the church that carries on the life of Jesus.

So I picked Acts for our initial time together on Sunday morning because I believe an examination of the pivotal points in the story of the early church will help us fall in love with what it means to be Christians who are on the road to mission with Jesus and members of a church that does what a church is supposed to do.

The Acts of the Apostles is the story of the birth and expansion of the early church. As such, it shares with us a unique framework around which to lead our congregation.

An interesting thing about Acts is the way it's constructed. It falls into six neat sections. And at the end of each section, Luke gives us a progress report on the spread of Christianity in that area of the world.

Acts 1:1–6:7 tell us of the progress of the church at Jerusalem and ends with "The word of God continued to spread; the number of the disciples increased greatly in Jerusalem, and a great many of the priests became obedient to the faith."

Acts 6:8–9:31 describes the spread of Christianity throughout Palestine and Samaria and ends with "Meanwhile the church throughout Judea, Galilee, and Samaria had peace and was built up . . . [and] increased in numbers."

> # Are you willing to do whatever it takes to push through to the limits of possibility?

Acts 9:32–12:24 includes the conversion of Paul, the extension to Antioch, and the reception of the Gentile Cornelius into the faith and ends with "The word of God continued to advance."

Acts 12:25–16:5 tells of the expansion of the church through Asia Minor and Galatia and ends with "So the churches were strengthened in the faith and increased in numbers daily."

Acts 16:6–19:20 describes the expansion of the church into Europe and ends with "So the word of the Lord grew mightily and prevailed."

Acts 19:21–28:31 ends with the arrival of Paul at Rome—the center of the known world at the time—and ends with "proclaiming the kingdom of God and teaching about the Lord Jesus Christ with all boldness and without hindrance."

I think you get the picture—Acts is about the spread of the church and the fulfillment of Acts 1:8, which is our anchor text for the next few months.

Many questions have been raised about Acts, such as:

- Why are so many things repeated and so many things we know from letters written by the Apostle Paul left out?
- Why do we have so few chronological points of reference?
- Why is it that Peter fades out of the picture after the fifteenth chapter?
- Why is it that Paul takes center stage after Acts 9?

Although no one really knows for sure the answers to these questions, I think Luke wrote only what the Holy Spirit wanted us to focus on—the fantastic story of the birth and rapid growth of the early church. In thirty short years, the church grew from an insignificant Jewish sect to a powerful force in the Roman Empire.

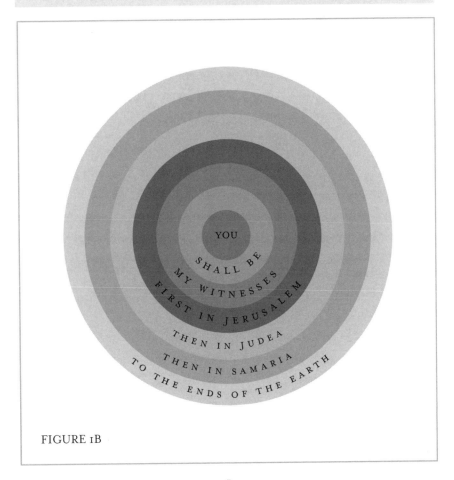

YOU
SHALL BE
MY WITNESSES
FIRST IN JERUSALEM
THEN IN JUDEA
THEN IN SAMARIA
TO THE ENDS OF THE EARTH

FIGURE 1B

uke also wanted to establish the spiritual authority of Paul, which was seriously under attack at the time. Every great moment must have an undisputed leader.

Acts provides essential background information for the churches Paul founded during the first sixty years of Christianity and the letters he wrote to them. Acts is a companion letter to Luke's Gospel and shows that Christianity was not a political threat to Rome but was the outworking of the Holy Spirit.

One thing is obvious in Acts—Luke wanted us to know more about Paul than any of the other apostles. I think the reason is simple—more than any other apostle, Paul did what all Christians are supposed to do—he spent his life sharing Jesus with lost people. And we should do the same.

## Acts 1:8

This text will be our anchor for the entire series of messages. Throughout the series, we will examine what it means to be an Acts 1:8 church in today's world. This one verse has been called by some "The Legacy of Christ."[4] Everything we know about the post-Resurrection Church of Jesus Christ was birthed on this day.

The setting for our text is Jerusalem, not long after the death and resurrection of Jesus. The disciples are hunkered down doing what Jesus had told them to do—wait for God to fill them with power. This power is called the Holy Spirit. Anytime the Holy Spirit is mentioned in Acts, the author is pointing to one simple truth—whatever we achieve as God's people isn't our doing: we accomplish it by God's power. That's one reason our mission can never be small and puny.

On that day, Jesus said, "I want you to be a witness of me, first in Jerusalem, then Judea, then Samaria, and then to the end of the world." I don't know how Jesus could be more clear—the mission of the church is to spread throughout the entire world. So our mission is also clear. We are to share our faith with the world and make a difference in our city. This is Christ's legacy to the world.

Over the next few months, I will refer to this text as "The Ever-widening Circle." We aren't called to take care of ourselves or build a huge institutional church. We are called to transform the world, beginning right here in our city and spreading throughout the state, the nation, and the world.

So let me share four axioms I try to live by. Perhaps they will show you how serious I am when I ask you to join me on this journey of transformation.

You may want to use each axiom in a PowerPoint slide on the screen.

### AXIOM ONE: IT'S ALL ABOUT JESUS CHRIST.

The goal of a real church is not to be an institution with charters and rules and regulations. The goal of the church is to bring people under the Lordship of Jesus Christ. Having a deep and personal relationship with Jesus is the ultimate goal of Christianity. Everything else is mere window dressing. When Christ is the head of the church, all petty stuff disappears. When people live under the Cross, they don't have time to sweat the small stuff.

Jesus said, "You shall be my witness." The Apostle Paul put it this way, "For no man can lay a foundation other than the one which is laid, which is Jesus Christ" (1 Cor. 3:11 NASB). In one of Peter's sermons, he says, "Salvation is found in no one else" (Acts 4:12 NIV). We will see this truth lived out over and over throughout the story in Acts. In fact, most—if not all—the stories in Acts are about how Jesus and the Holy Spirit transform lives.

You may want to spend some time on the meaning of the word *witness*. If so, here are some things you might consider.

In a legal sense, to be a *witness* is to give an account of one's personal experience, as in "I know this to be true."

*Witness* is not just about words; it's also about how we live. People come to Christ just by watching how some Christians live.

The word *witness* means martyr. Being a witness for Christ means being willing to sacrifice even our lives, if it comes to that.

### AXIOM TWO: THE ONLY WAY TO KNOW THE LIMITS OF OUR POSSIBILITY IS BY PUSHING THROUGH THEM TO THE IMPOSSIBLE.

Great Christians have the willpower and persistence to "push through" the normal and the everyday to the other side of normal and everyday issues. They never see impasses, only obstacles in the way—obstacles that have to be removed and overcome.[5] Spiritual giants understand the importance of resilience and perseverance. Like a dog with a bone, they push into areas of life that, on the surface, seem beyond their ability. They understand the power behind the early church— that the presence of the Holy Spirit makes anything possible. Until we believe that, we're really not the church of Jesus Christ.

Now, if we believe this axiom, two things are likely to happen to us on this mission. On the one hand, we might experience a horrible failure. This journey I'm asking you to join me on isn't any slam dunk. We could fall flat on our faces, because it's beyond our ability to pull off on our own. On the other hand, we might be tempted along the way to give up our mission before achieving it. Either one of which is where the "pushing through" comes into play. Let me share two stories with you.

Bil Cornelius is the pastor of one of the most successful church plants in the last decade. His church, Bay Area Fellowship, runs around seven thousand in worship after only twelve years. What most people don't know is that Bil's first experience in church planting ended in a dismal failure. But in the failure, Bil learned what not to do the next time around.

As a result, the mission statement of Bay Area is "Whatever It Takes." When I'm around Bil I get the feeling that his entire life centers around "Whatever It Takes," and I know from personal experience that his leaders sense this commitment in him.

> # The only way we can succeed is if God intervenes on behalf of the mission.

Steve Sjogren was the founding pastor of Cincinnati Vineyard. He left the church after twenty-some years of successful ministry to begin his coaching ministry. What most people don't know is that the first two years of his church plant were so unproductive that the average person would have quit. Steve had only a handful of people. But he believed deeply in his servant evangelism dream and continued cleaning toilets for businesses until the church exploded with people.

The mission I'm inviting you to join me in is far beyond our ability to achieve ourselves. The only way possible for us to succeed is for God to intervene on our behalf and for his Kingdom. This means we must be willing to fail or be scared out of our wits or be tested beyond our own faith endurance in order to achieve our mission. We must be willing to be in prayer for the mission every day. I'm asking you to join me on the ride of your life.

If your church is declining it is easy to say, "Anything would be better than what we're experiencing now." If your church is on a plateau you could say, "I know we've held our own the past decade, but we need to remember we are all ten years older, and the funerals are beginning to pile up." If you know what a mesa is and if more than 50 percent of your worshiping congregation is over 60, you could make a graph of the past decade or two showing the plateau and then having the line drop straight down to illustrate the age of the congregation. If your church is thriving, you could say, "Now is the time for us to pray about becoming a multi-site church or becoming a church-planting church."

I'm asking you to join me in pushing through the limits of our possibility to discover what is possible.

## AXIOM THREE: IT'S IN THE IMPOSSIBLE THAT GOD PROFOUNDLY CONFRONTS US.

Great Christians know that, even though God is found in the ordinary events in life and often uses those events for even greater things, we still experience God most profoundly when we enter the domain of the impossible. It's when we are totally stripped of our ability to perform or achieve that our dependence on God becomes crystal clear. One reason the average person never experiences the depths of God is because they never really venture out on faith. They never put themselves in the path of the impossible, where God is most likely to be.

The Bible tells the story about the day the disciples were on a lake and a great storm threatened to capsize the boat. Jesus appeared, walking on the water, and asked the disciple Peter to join him. It wasn't until Peter stepped out of the boat that he realized the awesome power of God (Matt. 14:22-34). Had he remained in the boat just imagine the experience he would have missed. I'm asking you to jump out of the boat with me and experience the awesome power of God.

You may want to look for some of the many videos about Peter stepping out of the boat during that storm. I love the one on YouTube with the funny ending (http://www.youtube.com/watch?v=WEInKgp47Bk). Take a look at it and when it's over ask your congregation which of the three they

11

would like to be like—Jesus, Peter, or the guy afraid of the bull? A serious video done well is at http://www.youtube.com/watch?v=itzIHD62Rno&NR=1. Focus on the message, "I want to trust you to do the impossible with our church. I know you want us to step out on faith." If you're a young church with lots of golfers, you may find a way to use this unusual video of Tiger Woods walking on water (even though now we all know that he doesn't): http://www.youtube.com/watch?v=FZ1st1Vw2kY&feature=related.

It's time some of us quit playing it safe and took a risk. We will never see the fulfillment of God's dream for this church unless we step out into the impossible. We simply can't settle for the routine. We need to place ourselves in positions where our only salvation is for God to intervene on our behalf. Prayer and reliance aren't just about getting bailed out of a situation. They're also about reaching our potential. Reliance on God taking action is embedded in this mission. We will not be alone if we follow God's commands.

AXIOM FOUR: GREAT CHRISTIANS ARE NEVER CONTENT WITH ANYTHING—
AT LEAST NOT UNTIL THE KINGDOM COMES ON EARTH.

Great Christians are never content with their life or leadership, no matter how good both are. We must develop a holy discontent with the status quo. We know there is always room to improve everything in life. Contentment to us must become a four-letter word.

Peter Drucker was an example of never being content with his leadership. Drucker died in 2005 at the age of 96; his last publication was in 2005. He never stopped learning and sharing. My favorite quotation of Drucker's is, "The best way to predict the future is to create it."[6] That's what we must do here—create the future that God has in store for us. God doesn't want our work to fail. God wants us to change this city.

You may want to use Moses and the burning bush experience to show how God can take an ordinary criminal and use him for purposes beyond his wildest dreams. And God can do the same with us (Exodus 3).

Great Christians live as if they have had a burning bush experience that is shaping all of their life and making it impossible for them to rest on their accomplishments. Sure, they are happy; but content, no. There's always another hill to climb, another spiritual war to be won.

So here is my question to you, "Do you have the courage to push through to the limits of your abilities and to live as if anything is possible if God is in it?"

If our vision isn't big enough to scare us, it's too small. If it isn't so big that there's no way we can accomplish it, it isn't God's vision; it's a goal. If we can accomplish it on our own, it isn't from God. God is found most fully in the impossible.

I read somewhere that we can never know our limits until we challenge ourselves to go beyond them. So I'm inviting you to join me in an impossible mission—not only a mission to turn around this church and help it grow but also a mission to transform the face of our city.[7]

You will need to be ready to embody this challenge. What kinds of small wins can you generate immediately in which people can experience the joy of transforming their community? In the first couple of months of my ministry, I manufactured a couple of small wins to encourage my potential leaders. They were small, but I knew I could pull them off, even though the leaders didn't think so. What small win can you pull off that your leaders don't think is possible? If you need some concrete ideas, visit www.servolution.org and www.servantevangelism.com. Also, consider reading the books written by the pastors behind those websites, Dino Rizzo's *Servolution* and Steve Sjogren's *Conspiracy of Kindness*.

Don't be afraid at this point to step up and lead. That is what God called you to do if you are a pastor or lay leader in your church. Left to their own, most churches will remain inwardly focused—that's the nature of sin. You must be willing to step out in front and challenge your people. Every vision in the Bible comes from an individual, not a committee. One of the reasons churches are declining is because they are run by committee instead of vision. You must change this in order for your church to grow.

## Three Essentials in Transformation

Throughout this series, you should notice three crucial ingredients of any form of transformation. If any one of the following three ingredients is missing, transformation doesn't happen. You would do well sometime in the early stages of preaching on Acts to share the following information, in whatever fashion best fits your situation. You need to ground your people in the way God works through a church.

---

# Three Essentials in Transformation:
# The Holy Spirit
# Transformational Preaching
# Committed People

---

*The power and presence of the Holy Spirit.* Throughout Acts, we will encounter the Holy Spirit moving through the leaders and churches. And every time the Spirit shows up, we see one of the following—chaos, growth, accountability, or comfort.

*Transformational preaching.* Never underestimate the power of preaching and teaching. Acts is full of examples of what happens when Jesus is proclaimed.

*The role of the committed people of God.* Not everyone in your church will respond to the challenge and be part of the solution. But some will, and those folks are a key to the future. I never would have been able to turn the church around without them. Many times, they stood in the gap between the opposition and me and took the heat. Their prayers and actions made the difference. Transformation can't be done without the cooperation of the spiritual leaders.

**Warning:** Not everyone will take part. Some will always resist, and some may even resist in evil ways and try to do to you what the Pharisees did to Jesus.

### Step Out on Faith

I ended my first Sunday morning message with this challenge, and I encourage you to do something similar as soon as you feel you're ready. Somewhere along the way of transformation, you have to gather a team of supportive lay people, especially if you are in a declining established church.

Next Sunday we will examine this impossible mission in detail and see how God says it plays out. God is calling us to follow him to the ends of the earth. How? The book of Acts will be our guide for this journey. I will be using Acts over the next few months because it lays out the blueprint for explosive growth and transformation of our city.

So I'm asking anyone who wants to join me in developing a church of thousands and transforming our city to join me at the parsonage tonight at seven o'clock, and we'll talk about it.

Twelve of the thirty-seven people present that Sunday showed up. I met with these folks every Friday night for the next eight months or so. We prayed; we read Acts; and we covenanted to support one another as we birthed a new church. What happened during the next twenty-four years couldn't have happened without our study of Acts, the presence of the Holy Spirit, and these brave folks who prayed for and supported one another through it all. The same is true with you and your church. I encourage you to end your message with the mission God has laid on your heart.

## What to Do with This Group

The following is to be used only if you invite a group to your home and they actually show up.

First, don't think in terms of traditional teaching. What this group does together isn't a course in how to be a disciple. Instead, here's what I would do.

The main thing you do with this group is hang out with them so they can catch your passion and DNA. Any way you can, spend time with them around your vision for the church. Do whatever will work—eat together, play together, share communion together, walk the neighborhood and pray for each house. Do whatever helps them see your heart.

To understand why you should do this, just look at what Jesus did with the disciples—he hung out with them for three years. He was the curriculum, and so are you. A quick reading of the New Testament shows a pattern—after being called, all of the great names we remember from the story spent time being prepared by simply following their mentors around. Even Paul spent time with Barnabas, learning his trade in Antioch.

The time will come when you need this group to be able to step up to the plate and continue the work you've begun. You don't have the luxury of thinking you can do this alone or that the work will continue after you're gone unless you prepare this group.

Study Acts part of the time and make sure you focus on your vision. You ought to be able to bring your vision into every passage you study. But don't make the mistake of turning your time with this group into a mere study period.

Begin the time by exploring the movement and antics of the church in the Acts of the Apostles. Spend time talking about the results of the Holy Spirit appearing among the Christians. Look at how the church hunkered down in the early chapters and how it took folks like Philip and Peter taking the initiative to move beyond the confines of the church.

Then, begin to trace the outward movement of Paul and how the Jerusalem church tried to stop the movement from going beyond the legalism of the Jewish law. Explore how that compares to what the church does today.

You should now be several weeks into your time together. Begin to pray that God gives your church the will to move out into the Gentile world. In a week or two, suggest that on Saturday the group meet for an outing into the Gentile world. Options include a Servant Evangelism project found at www.kindness.com or door-to-door asking what the people need most from the churches in their area. Begin to address any ideas you might have uncovered in the door-to-door. If you did an SE project, have one of the participants tell how meaningful it was to them. Then ask the church to set aside one Saturday a month for such a project for the whole church.

Continue exploring Acts with the group. Watch how new leadership emerges in the birth and growth of the church. Talk with the group about opening their homes for a small group study like the ones done in the first century and see what happens. You might be surprised.

# NOTES

1. You can find a video of the song at http://www.youtube.com/watch?v=RfHnzYE-HAow. You can also find a decent synopsis of the musical at http://en.wikipedia.org/wiki/Man_of_La_Mancha.

2. Go to the support page for "What to Do in the First Year of a New Pastorate."

3. Go to the support page for "The Risks of Turning Around a Church."

4. *The New American Commentary: Acts* (Nashville: Holman Reference, 1992), p. 83.

5. I wrote about this some time ago in my book *Leadership on the OtherSide* (Nashville: Abingdon, 2000).

6. "Peter Drucker," BrainyQuote.com. Xplore Inc., May 5, 2010. http://www.brainy quote.com/quotes/quotes/p/peterdruck131600.html.

7. See the support page for a turnaround graphic.

CHAPTER 2

# AN EVER-WIDENING CIRCLE

## KEY IDEA

GOD WANTS US TO KNOW TODAY THAT HIS DESIRE
FOR HIS CHURCH IS THAT IT SHOULD SPREAD AND SPREAD
UNTIL THE ENTIRE CREATION BOWS BEFORE JESUS THE CHRIST.
(INSERT YOUR OWN WORD FOR GOD.)

Remember, this could be several messages.

**Acts 1:8**

*"But you will receive power when the Holy Spirit comes on you; and you will be
my witnesses in Jerusalem, and in all Judea and Samaria, and to the ends of the
earth." (NIV)*

As I mentioned last Sunday, I'm anchoring this series in Acts 1:8, and I'm
doing so for three reasons.[1] First, it contains what the early church considered to
be the last will and testament of Jesus. Nothing could be more binding than the last
words of our resurrected Lord.

My father died before I could get to the hospital. When I got there, my mother
handed me a piece of paper with some words written on it. They were the last
words my father wanted me to hear. I still have those words in my wallet. I will never
forget them. Families who have experienced the last words of a loved one know
the importance of such words, and no one with any heart can ignore them. The
same is true for Christians—the last words of our Lord have precedence over
everything. We dare not ignore them.

Second, this text contains the prime directive of the church, which I call the
Basic Law of Congregational Life (BLCL).[2] This "law" is the reality that "churches
grow when they intentionally reach out to others, and churches die when all they
do is take care of themselves."

> # The Basic Law of Congregational Life:
> Churches grow when they intentionally reach out to others, and churches die when all they do is take care of themselves.

How can the Scriptures be any clearer than this text? Jesus says, "Be my witness." The BLCL challenges congregations with the primary reasons churches decline—self-centeredness and feelings of entitlement. This text is a reminder that life does not revolve around us or our church. Life is centered on how we treat the stranger whom God sends our way. Growing churches are more concerned about people than the preservation of the institution or making sure there is money in the bank for a rainy day. Dying churches focus on their own needs and look for ways to merely survive.

Third, I begin with this text because it lays the foundation for any and all authentic power within Christianity—the Holy Spirit. It's not until we are filled with the Spirit that we are able, with God's help, to move our church forward into an impossible journey. What we are to accomplish in this church will not be our own doing; it will be the doing of the Holy Spirit working through us.

## The Ever-widening Circle

I call this text the Ever-widening Circle because it eliminates any doubts about the role of the church.[3] Just look at the graphic. It begins with "you" and then continues to expand until it extends to the ends of the earth. The role of the church is to turn itself outward to the world and witness to Jesus Christ "unto the ends of the earth."

God has called every one of us to be a witness to Jesus in everything we do. Look at the text—*"You will be my witnesses."* Jesus doesn't ask us to be his witnesses. He says we *will* be his witnesses. All through Acts, the word *witness* is tied to discipleship. A true disciple is always a witness to Jesus—not to God, not to the church, not to our denomination, but to Jesus. *"You will be my witnesses."*

The word *martyr* literally means "witness," and throughout Acts the word *witness* came to be synonymous with suffering and death. We may not be called upon to literally die for our faith, but we will be called upon to sacrifice for our faith. We will be asked to put self aside on behalf of the mission God has given us.

### JERUSALEM

First, we are to be a witness to Jerusalem. I take *Jerusalem* to be the church. Jerusalem was the spiritual center of the world for Jews in Jesus' day. Every male

Jew was expected to make a pilgrimage to Jerusalem between one and three times a year. Jerusalem was the center of their religion, much like the local church is to Christians today.

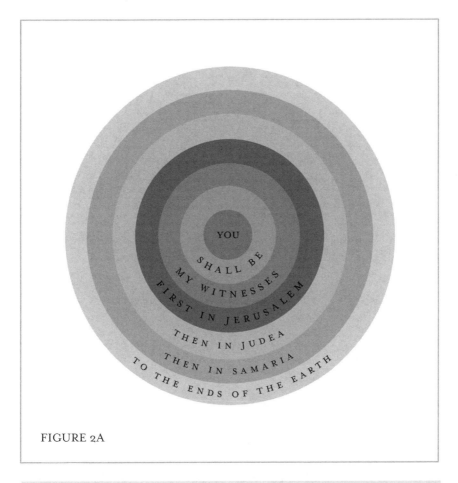

FIGURE 2A

I would make this graphic the key visual throughout the series. Put it on every slide, or at least at the beginning of each message. You might want to go to Google Earth and use that site to give people an up-close view of Jerusalem and Judea. If you have broadband access in the worship center, you may want to demonstrate it live, but only if you or someone in your booth really knows how and can do it quickly.

So I need to be clear—reaching out to the world in no way minimizes the importance of our church. Our church is the center of the impossible mission. Our church must remain healthy and strong in order for the mission to reach its potential. So there is no way I'll allow our outreach to jeopardize our church in any way. But remember the Basic Law of Congregational Life: "churches grow when they intentionally reach out to others, and churches die when all they do is take care of themselves." We must remain strong at home, but we must also use our strength on behalf of others.

## JUDEA

Second, we are to be a witness to Judea. Judea was the area of the world that surrounded Jerusalem. As such, Judea represents the area surrounding our church.

One of the great failures of modern-day Christianity is its failure to see its social and redemptive responsibility to the city. The kingdom of God goes beyond the local church and envelops all of life. A thriving church focuses on the city and spends time figuring out ways to help and transform it.

As Jesus wept over Jerusalem, so our churches should give of themselves to their city.

Why not mark off a section of your community and begin to pray for its salvation?

At this point, you might want to explore some of the city-reaching movements underway today. If so, go to http://churchconsultations.com/resources/faqs-resources-and-info/c/city-reaching/city-reaching-organizations/.

You might also want to do some further reading on city-reaching. If so, here are three good books—Dennison, *City Reaching*; Greenway, *Cities*; Meeks, *The First Urban Christians*.

## SAMARIA

Third, we are to be a witness to Samaria. The Samaritans were the outcasts of their day—people nobody wanted. So Jesus is telling us we aren't the church until we reach out to the unloved and unwanted of our day.

O r you may want to interpret Samaria as your state in the concentric circles reaching out into the world. There is no reason you could not use both outcast and state as examples of the reach of the church.

I'll never forget pastoring at my first United Methodist church. I was right out of seminary and green behind the gills. One of the first serious conversations I had with a member of the church was with a board member. During our first conversation, he took me to a railroad track that cut the small town in two and said, "You see those tracks? You're not to go beyond them because we don't want *those* people in our church." *Those* people were the very poor Hispanics. He knew who his Samaritan was, and he was not about to lower himself. He was far from the Kingdom even though he was a pillar of the church.

I s your church inclusive? Or has it targeted some people as "not welcome"?

## THE WORLD

Fourth, we are to be a witness to the whole world. Our church must be involved in world missions. It doesn't matter how much we reach out, there's always more to be done. We must believe that, with God's help, there is no limit to our ministry—it's an ever-widening reality.

The message is clear. Our witness is to begin at home and spread out to the ends of the world. The church is not the church unless it reaches out beyond its own four walls and embraces all races. Acts 1:8 lays the biblical foundation of the Great Commission.

But here's the kicker: the ends of the earth were never reached in Acts. The goal of Christ's legacy is never completed. At the end of Acts, we will see that the author left the story open-ended. That's where we come in. Our role, and the role of every generation, is to do our part in fulfilling the goal of taking the good news to the entire world. In taking that role, we become partners with God in fulfilling the mission begun by Jesus. The story of Acts is now our story. And I want us to write that story here and now.

23

You can find more information about the Ever-widening Circle in my books *The Church Growth Handbook* and *The Complete Ministry Audit.*[4]

To support this text, you may want to make reference to the stories of Philip in Acts 8.

### Acts 8:4-8

*Now those who were scattered went from place to place, proclaiming the word. Philip went down to the city of Samaria and proclaimed the Messiah to them. The crowds with one accord listened eagerly to what was said by Philip, hearing and seeing the signs that he did, for unclean spirits, crying with loud shrieks, came out of many who were possessed; and many others who were paralyzed or lame were cured. So there was great joy in that city.*

The following text again supports the emphasis on affecting the city.

### Acts 8:26-29

*Then an angel of the Lord said to Philip, "Get up and go toward the south to the road that goes down from Jerusalem to Gaza." (This is a wilderness road.) So he got up and went. Now there was an Ethiopian eunuch, a court official of the Candace, queen of the Ethiopians, in charge of her entire treasury. He had come to Jerusalem to worship and was returning home; seated in his chariot, he was reading the prophet Isaiah. Then the Spirit said to Philip, "Go over to this chariot and join it."*

These stories contain the first attempts of the early church to reach out beyond Jerusalem. Prior to Philip's time, the strategy of the early church included the same mistake most churches still make today—to hunker down and wait for the world to come to it.

The church at Jerusalem is a good example. It stayed home, hunkered down, and had to be subsidized by the new churches founded by Paul.

There will be more about this later in the series.

Be sure to discuss how difficult it is for the church to remain outwardly focused. Even the church at Jerusalem began to focus inward. If that could happen so soon after Christ's death, how easy it must be for churches today to turn inward. I think it is helpful and defusing for your people to know that even some of the disciples found it easier to stay within the safety of the four walls. It's just easier to focus inward on what one is familiar with than to move outward into unknown territory.

I spent a week exploring each of the outer rings in the graphic, and then took the congregation into the importance of world missions. Since my tribe (UMC) had limited world missions mostly to agricultural, medical, and disaster help, I had to emphasize that true world missions included both spreading the good news and giving a cup of cold water.

## EVANGELISM AND SOCIAL JUSTICE

As I worked through this text, I realized that some of my folk were guilty of separating evangelism from social justice. They welcomed the Samaritan, but they saw no problem with missionaries being little more than social missionaries whose goal was to feed the body in the hope it would also feed the soul. I had to make it clear to my flock that you can't feed the soul if you don't feed the body; and it doesn't do any good to feed the body if you don't feed the soul. Depending on your situation, you may want to spend an entire message on this subject.

The separation of social justice and evangelism is one of the worst forms of heresy in the history of Christianity. The long-standing fight between liberal and conservative Christianity[5] is one of the major blights on Christianity. It has truncated the church to the point that, in many cases, the church is a useless piece of junk that should be discarded. To say one is more important than the other is to discredit the words of Jesus found in the Great Commandment and the Great Commission. Social justice and evangelism are simply two sides of the same coin. One without the other is vain, stupid, and downright useless.

> You can't feed the soul if you don't feed the body; and it doesn't do any good to feed the body if you don't feed the soul.

Over the years I've heard many conversations about which is more important, evangelism or social justice. As if one could choose? Such stupidity! Such lack of understanding of the gospel! You can't choose one over the other and be a follower of Jesus. Not possible! Both are required for a whole gospel. Reductionism has hurt our witness over and over through the centuries. It's time we quit truncating the gospel.

I've also heard this argument: "Evangelism isn't always social justice, but social justice is always evangelism."[6] I don't buy this argument either. I've seen too many people use such an argument as an excuse not to verbalize the gospel when the time is right. I've dealt with a lot of church people who want to "do good" but have no interest in people coming to faith. And you know what Jesus said about being "good" (Luke 18:19).

For more about this, see "The Jesus Manifesto," developed by Leonard Sweet and Frank Viola, two Christian leaders who in some ways could not be more different but who transcended those differences to help us effectively hold evangelism and social justice together in a faithful perspective.[7]

I'm repeatedly baffled by the way so many churches do mission work without any reference to Jesus Christ. What they do is often no different from what a Lions Club or a Rotary Club might do. To give a cup of cold water without the name of Jesus attached to it is little more than what any good charity does. Christians have to go another step somewhere along the way. We have what no other group has to offer—the salvation of the world. To flinch from that belief is to deny the very essence of our faith.

To this day, I believe this early preaching about evangelism and social justice laid the foundation for our church becoming one of the premier churches in the U.S. when it came to combining social justice and evangelism.

### Acts 2:1-13

*When the day of Pentecost had come, they were all together in one place. And suddenly from heaven there came a sound like the rush of a violent wind, and it filled the entire house where they were sitting. Divided tongues, as of fire, appeared among them, and a tongue rested on each of them. All of them were filled with the Holy Spirit and began to speak in other languages, as the Spirit gave them ability. . . . All were amazed and perplexed, saying to one another, "What does this mean?" But others sneered and said, "They are filled with new wine."*

My emphasis here is on the relationship between being a witness to Jesus Christ in Acts 1:8 and having the power of the Holy Spirit to go before us. You may want to make this an entire message, and if so, you should focus on the power the Spirit brings to the actual mission.

Also, you may want to diffuse the issue of tongues. If I were going to use this text as the subject of an entire message, I would use the analogy of what I experienced once in an airport. I was eating a sandwich in one of those dining areas every airport has when I overheard a group behind me speaking in German. Across the aisle from me, a couple was speaking in French. To my right, a foursome was speaking in Japanese, and in the distance, I could hear a language being spoken that I did not know. All were being spoken at once; I could not understand a word any of them were saying, but we all had one thing in common—we all would soon board a plane. That's close to what happened on the day of Pentecost.

Of course, any way you try to minimize the miraculous will cause you more problems than it is worth when it comes to transformation. It is better to stay focused on the power of the Spirit as it relates to the mission of your church. The miracle was a demonstration of the Spirit's power and presence. As they understood one another through the Spirit's power, so too are we able to do things beyond our belief through the Spirit's power.

You may want to spend some time on the subject of the Holy Spirit in order to help people understand you're talking about not some spooky entity but rather God's presence in the world after Jesus ascended. Since there are so many different ways to interpret the role and meaning of the Holy Spirit, I leave the interpretation up to you. Just remember that whatever interpretation you arrive at, it must be connected with the rest of the verse, which certainly ties the role of the Holy Spirit to the growth of the church.

Jesus tells his disciples to stay put and not to do anything but hang out in a room until the Holy Spirit comes. Jesus doesn't want us to act without the Holy Spirit.

> Do a search of the word *spirit* in the book of Acts, and you will discover what the first followers of Jesus were empowered to do by the Spirit (such as preach with convincing power, grow the church, convert, baptize, engage in faithful accountability, heal, revive, and so forth).

Effective and authentic faith is explosive, uncontrollable, and spontaneous. Every time the Holy Spirit moved in Acts, people were upset, everything was turned upside down, and nothing made rational sense. How are you going to feel when we allow the Holy Spirit to break loose in our church and people begin acting differently and thousands of people give their lives to Christ?

Faith has little to do with the rational and predictable. My ministry among you will be explosive, spiritual, and I hope supernatural. God's will for us is to step out in faith, even if we don't have the money.

(You have to realize this was a restart church that was virtually bankrupt, both morally and financially.)

> For stuck churches to grow, they have to move out of their comfort zone. People have to change.

Too many churches play it too close to the vest. They go so far out of their way with checks and balances to ensure nothing bad happens that nothing good ever happens either. Christ didn't die so the church could play it safe. It's time our church shook things up a bit. It's time we did some things we've never done before. One of the most offensive statements to the Holy Spirit is, "We've never done it that way before."

For stuck churches to grow, they have to move out of their comfort zone. People have to change. It's just a natural part of doing business with the Holy Spirit. So buckle up.

Of course, we aren't asked to do this alone or in our own power. That's the primary point of the text—whatever God asks us to do, he does so in the assurance that he will also give us the power of the Spirit to make it happen.

### OUTSIDE IN

The advent of the Holy Spirit was so powerful that not only was it felt by the disciples, it caught the attention of people on the streets. They were drawn to the house where the disciples had gathered. They were astonished by what was happening. But some mocked.

And God wants that to happen with our church here, today. When we are filled with God's Spirit, people will be drawn to us and the church will grow. Of course, there will also be those naysayers.

Many pastors are surprised by how growth brings out naysayers. You'd think people would be happy with growth, but many aren't. It upsets the balance of power and makes it harder to control what happens.

You and I must avoid the mockery of the scoffer who explains everything in empirical terms and open ourselves up to the unexpected movement of God in our world. We must not give way to the fear of not-so-committed people. We must find leaders who are willing to trust God for the impossible. We may not be able to convince everyone; that's not our responsibility. Our responsibility is to receive the power from God and make his presence known in the world. I trust you are ready to receive God's power.

## Warning!

I think it is good wisdom to give notice to the "controllers" that true spirituality is not exhibited by people who are fearful of their church growing because they will lose control of what happens. Sooner or later, these folks have to be challenged and called out. If you are in your first six months as pastor of the church, this is the best time to challenge them.

Freedom, spontaneity, and flexibility in reaching out to the nonbelievers are at the heart of the biblical church. Then I would ask, "How well does this describe the way this church functions?" You see, being new, I could play dumb and, at the same time, open a can of worms, if one does exist. But I have couched my challenge in the Scriptures, not in some issue that can be hotly debated.

You may want to look at an article I wrote entitled "On Not Being Nice for the Sake of the Gospel." It is one of the most requested articles I've ever written. If you need it, it will give you ammunition to use on the controllers. Keep in mind they do not have the right to stand in the way of what God wants for every church—the growth of God's people and the spread of the Kingdom.[8]

## Taking It Home

Keep in mind that you can't traverse this path alone. You need the support of the leaders. So start looking for those who will walk this path with you. This group should already be traveling with you if you followed the path laid out for you in the first message—the one where you invite people to meet and go on the journey with you. For at least the next eight months, your Friday nights should be occupied with meeting with those whose eyes lit up and who leaned forward with anticipation when you preached that first message. If you are married, ask your spouse to notice whose eyes light up and whose heads nod when you preach these messages. Make sure you reach out to them. These are the people who are pregnant with hope and possibility, and your job is to be a spiritual midwife for them and help them give birth to a concrete movement of Jesus in your community.

# NOTES

1. For a short PowerPoint presentation that might give you some ideas how to use Google Earth to dramatize Acts 1:8, go to the support page.

2. You can find more on the Basic Law of Congregational Life in my book *The Church Growth Handbook*.

3. See the support page for an Ever-widening Circle graphic.

4. Both of these books can be purchased from Abingdon Press.

5. http://www.missionalpeople.com/2009/06/mission-social-justice-or-evangelism.

6. http://whateverisgood.blogspot.com/2008/03/evangelism-and-social-justice.html.

7. http://frankviola.wordpress.com/2009/06/22/a-jesus-manifesto-by-leonard-sweet-and-frank-viola/.

8. http://churchconsultations.com/index.php?id=3064.

# CHAPTER 3

# THE TWO IMPERATIVES OF THE EARLY CHURCH AND THE CENTRALITY OF JESUS

**KEY IDEA**
A WILLINGNESS TO SHARE OUR FAITH DEPENDS
ON HOW DEVOTED AND OBEDIENT WE ARE TO JESUS.

.    Previously, I shared with you the Ever-widening Circle, which forms the anchor for this series, and we looked at what I call the "Basic Law of Congregational Life."

Today, I want to emphasize two christological imperatives I find in the actions of the earliest Christians—*devotion* and *obedience* to Jesus, God's anointed one. It's our devotion and obedience that will help us understand the implications of God's claim on our lives and help us move out of our comfort zone and transform our city.

## The Centrality of Jesus

Many established pastors are notorious for not knowing what to do with Jesus and often try to separate the Jesus of Nazareth from the Christ of faith—as if Jesus were a reality and the Christ of faith only a myth (in the best sense of the word). In my preaching, I refused to make any distinction between the historical Jesus and the Christ of faith. To call Jesus "the Christ" is simply to acknowledge that Jesus is God's anointed one, whom we call "Lord."

In order for us to go forward in this series, we have to settle the "Jesus issue." According to Paul, Jesus is the focal point of all preaching and teaching. Paul said,

"For I determined not to know any thing among you, save Jesus Christ, and him crucified" (1 Cor. 2:2 KJV). Paul was not talking about a mere man here. He was referring to the Son of God.

---

# Jesus is Lord and Christ.

---

Emil Brunner coined a phrase that has stuck with me all these years. He referred to Jesus as the "scandal of particularity." The early Greeks thought of Jesus as a stumbling block or a scandal because Christians proclaimed that the living God came among a particular people, the Jews, and took on human flesh in the particular man Jesus.

The same is true today. Many people try to make Jesus out to be just a man, but in doing so, they violate every teaching of the Scriptures. In order for the first-century Christians to give their lives that we might hear the good news today, they had to believe that, in Jesus, God has come to redeem a world in need of a spiritual bath. You've heard it said many times, but it's still the most trusted truth in the universe—Jesus is the salvation of all creation, and that includes you and me. Paul wrote to the Philippian church, "Every tongue should confess that Jesus Christ is Lord, to the glory of God the Father" (Phil. 2:11). We've already heard Peter proclaim, "Therefore let all the house of Israel know assuredly that God has made this Jesus, whom you crucified, both Lord and Christ" (Acts 2:36 NKJV). For Jesus to be Lord and Christ means that everything about our lives, from morals to faith, depends on our relationship with Jesus.

You may want to make an entire message on the centrality of Jesus. If so, you may want to explore the writings of Brunner, Barth, Newbegin, and others. I chose not to because where I was preaching in Texas, there wasn't the need to dwell long on the subject.

### Acts 2:14-40; Acts 4:12

*There is salvation in no one else, for there is no other name under heaven given among mortals by which we must be saved.* (Acts 4:12)

Since this chapter is a departure from the overall theme of reaching out, I felt it was imperative for this congregation to get right with one another and with God before stepping out into the world and inviting their networks to attend worship or a small group. If your church is clear on the lordship of Jesus Christ, you may want to either skip this section or reduce it to one message. If devotion and obedience to Jesus aren't evident in the lives of your leaders, you need to spend at least one or two messages on the subject of devotion and obedience to Jesus.

Peter's sermon follows on the heels of the coming of the Holy Spirit. His purpose was to explain the implications of what had just happened minutes before. The response of the people to the advent of the Holy Spirit was so powerful, Peter had to first convince the people the disciples weren't drunk because it was only nine in the morning.

Then Peter proceeded to lay the foundation for the rest of God's mission on earth. That's how important this sermon is to the history of Christianity. One thing stands out above all else—Jesus is the cornerstone of God's mission in this world. "Therefore let all Israel be assured of this: God has made this Jesus, whom you crucified, both Lord and Christ" (Acts 2:36 NIV). Jesus is so central to their mission that the earliest Christians were referred to as "followers of the Way." It's not until chapter 11 of the book of Acts that these followers of Jesus are finally called "Christians" (see Acts 11:26). And the term *Christian* appears only that one time in the entire New Testament. But over and over again in the book of Acts, the followers of Jesus were known as followers of "the Way" (Acts 19:9; 19:23; 22:4; 24:14; 24:22). And, of course, the Scriptures tell us that "I [Jesus] am the way, and the truth, and the life" (John 14:6).

## JESUS IS THE MISSION

In Acts 4, the Sanhedrin, the highest legislative and judicial body in Israel, convened to question Peter and John about their preaching. It was there Peter preached his defense of Jesus and shared with them that salvation came only through Jesus.

In my early years of consulting, I spent a lot of time in the Northeast. I can't tell you how many laypeople would privately say to me, "Thank you for speaking the name of Jesus. It's been so long since we've heard his name in the pulpit."

On one occasion, after four days of consulting with a church, as the pastor dropped me off at the airport, he asked, "Several times you've mentioned a personal relationship with Jesus Christ. What do you mean by that?" If we are going to call ourselves Christians, then Jesus Christ must be a central part of our faith.

When you remove Jesus from the conversation, there is no conversation worth pursuing for the church.

Perhaps you have had some similar experiences. You should share them here.

## GOD IS MEANINGLESS WITHOUT JESUS

The world of Jesus' day, like our world today, was a pagan society.[1] By that, I mean we live in a world where many gods vie for the devotion and obedience of people. In such a world, to ask someone if he or she believes in god is a meaningless question. The public doesn't have a clue which god you are talking about. Especially since the popularity of media stars, like Oprah, who preach a smorgasbord type of god: a little of this and a little of that, mix it all together, and behold—the god of Oprah emerges.

Because of people like Oprah, people have no clue what is meant when they hear the word *god*. Therefore, it's important that we distinguish which god we are talking about. Like the people of the Old Testament who talked about "the God of Abraham, Isaac, and Jacob," we must talk about the God of Jesus Christ.

Paul understood this fact, so the focus of his preaching was clearly on Jesus and not God, because no one would know which god he was talking about.[2] The same is true today. We have to talk about the God of Jesus Christ, or no one will know which god we are talking about.

But many people disagree with me on this point, especially mainline people (most of whom lead dying churches) who want to keep Jesus on the sideline and focus on God. In a pagan world, that's suicide because, believe me, the devotees to the other gods know the difference between their god and your God.

### Acts 2:30, 36

*Since he was a prophet, he knew that God had sworn with an oath to him that he would put one of his descendants on his throne. . . . Therefore let the entire house of Israel know with certainty that God has made him both Lord and Messiah, this Jesus whom you crucified.*

> Based on the Scriptures, I wanted to nail down two clear imperatives for the local church: the earliest churches' devotion and obedience to Jesus Christ. He was both their Lord and Savior.

The early church was clearly christological, both in its obedience and in its devotion. Its message was about God as experienced in Jesus. And they refused to make any separation between "Jesus" and "Christ."

---

## Two Imperatives:
- Devotion to Jesus
- Obedience to Jesus

---

To say Jesus sits on God's throne and to call him Lord and Christ is to separate Jesus from all other humans and to equate him with God. As such, he commands our devotion and obedience.

This is one of the non-negotiables of the faith. Jesus is both our Lord and Savior, or he is nothing to us. Our entire faith and belief system rests on these two imperatives.

### DEVOTION TO JESUS

In the early stages of Christianity, devotion to God and to Jesus was common. Throughout Acts, the term *Lord* is used twice as many times for Jesus as for God. The explicit devotion to Jesus is unparalleled in Jewish literature. Jesus was worshiped in prayers where people prayed directly to him (Acts 7:59), in invocations to intervene in life's affairs that one could only attribute to a god (in 1 Cor. 5), and in baptisms (Acts 8:16; 10:48). In the Lord's Supper (1 Cor. 11:20), Jesus played a role that hitherto had been reserved only for the gods. In addition, Jesus was worshiped directly through hymns (Eph. 5:19) and in prophecy (2 Cor. 12:9). Why? Because Jesus' first faithful followers were clear on this: Jesus was and is the very revelation of the living God.

Jesus was revered and prayed to so often that, over time, the church felt it necessary to convene several councils to determine what the relationship of Jesus was to God.[3] After all, monotheism is at the heart of both Judaism and Christianity. You know the final verdict—Jesus was very God and very human. Needless to say, Jesus is at the center of any form of authentic Christianity.

## OBEDIENCE TO JESUS

Obedience to Jesus is a natural result of such devotion. Obedience to God can be found only through Jesus.

But what does this obedience look like? Sitting in a pew? Going to committees? Christ didn't die for such nonsense. If we follow Jesus' example, we know that real Christianity begins when we exit this building. Christ didn't die so we could sit and soak in comfortable pews; he died so we could make disciples of all nations (Matt. 28:18).

One of the last stories about Jesus occurs in the last chapter of Luke's Gospel, where we find two guys walking away from Jerusalem to Emmaus. Along the way, the resurrected Jesus joins them, and they have a conversation. I don't think Luke dropped in this story by chance. Jerusalem was the religious center of Jewish life, and Emmaus was a Roman garrison filled with Gentiles.[4] Just so we're all clear—the word *Gentile* meant anyone who wasn't Jewish. I hope you're beginning to see the picture. One of Luke's last images of Jesus is him walking away from the Jewish faith and into our Gentile world. For us to follow Jesus means we must be on the road to mission with people who have yet to hear and accept the good news.

Obedience to Jesus is just another way of saying that the earliest church saw its reason for existence to be missional. To be obedient to Jesus was to do what Jesus did—leave the religious center called the Sanctuary and relate to the nonbeliever and challenge the professional Christian. To be obedient to Jesus was to be with him on the road to mission, to be moving away from Jerusalem and toward Emmaus. All theology and ministry are defined by missions. Every Christian has the potential to be a missionary of Jesus Christ. Think about it. All people who call themselves Christians should consider themselves to be missionaries!

The focus of authentic ministry is always more outward than inward. The pinnacle of Christian maturity is when our primary concern is the salvation of the world, rather than the entitlements that come with church membership. That's why I will spend 80 percent of my time helping the congregation transform San Antonio, instead of spending most of my time visiting them in their homes or in the hospital. I told them they could have one day a week for meetings and that day could only be Friday through Sunday.

Throughout my message to them about devotion and obedience, I continually weaved these two points: the mission of the church is to share Jesus with the world, and to remove Jesus from the conversation is to cease being the church.

## THE KICKER

Now here's the kicker—before obedience and devotion to Jesus can happen, repentance must take place.

When the people asked what they could do in response to God's great act in raising up Jesus, Peter said, "Repent and be baptized . . . in the name of Jesus Christ for the forgiveness of your sins. And you will receive the gift of the Holy Spirit" (Acts 2:38 NIV).

Repentance always precedes devotion and obedience to Jesus and the coming of the Holy Spirit into a person's life. Peter made this very clear in his message on the Day of Pentecost (Acts 2:38).

I know, repentance isn't a common word in most churches, but it's essential to having the kind of leaders who will stand in the gap when the going gets tough.

If you are in a dying church, the going will get tough before getting better when you try to turn it around.

So how does repentance work?

Jesus said, "I am not come to call the righteous, but sinners to repentance" (Matt. 9:13 KJV). Jesus soundly declared the message in his day: "repent and believe the gospel." Repentance and faith are inseparable and occur simultaneously in a sinner's heart; you cannot have one without the other.

So what is repentance? It's a change in heart, mind, and action toward God and his commands. It literally means to "turn around" and do a 180. Remember that chart I showed you about the trend of our congregation? Do you want to keep going in the same direction? Another year like the last few years, and we can close the door. You fill in information about your situation. If not, then it's time for a 180; it's time to turn around. It's time to change our hearts, our minds, and our actions. It's time to repent.

In true biblical repentance, three things must occur.

- We have to see ourselves as we really are—lost, ruined, and guilty—and ac-knowledge our sin. If we are to join Jesus on the road to mission, we have to acknowledge our sin. It is that simple. Each one of us is a sinner for one rea-son or another. For some, it's personal; for others, it's how we keep the church in an uproar; but all of us have sinned, and we have no part in Jesus until we confess it, ask for forgiveness, and turn our lives around.

- We must reach a place where we are horrified by our condition and cry out to God for help. It's not enough to feel sorry for what we've done or become. We must hate what we've become. Repentance comes about through the con-victing power of the Spirit of God and causes a change in our attitude, our actions, and our affection toward Jesus Christ.

- We must abandon sin and throw ourselves on God's mercy. Let's not be fooled—repentance involves turning away and forsaking sin. Repentance is not only a heart broken for sin, but also from sin. We must forsake what we would have God forgive.

Depending on your situation, you may want to use this section about repentance in the next chapter instead. Read the section in the next chapter before you decide whether to use this section here or at all.

## Now What?

The ending to this message depends on the condition of your church lead-ers, as well as your theology. You may need to have a call for repentance that leads to devotion and obedience to Jesus, or you may want to skip the repen-tance section and end simply with a call for devotion and obedience to Jesus. It all depends on the present attitude of your congregation and your theology.

I choose to focus more on the devotion and obedience and show how if those are present in our lives, it is easier to be part of God's impossible mission. If you know opposition to the church reaching out is coming, you may want to name it and call for repentance, especially if you are a church planter or restart pastor.

If you have some people in your church who have been opposed to every new idea but have had a recent turnaround because of a change of heart, ask one of them to end this message with a five-minute testimony of what God can do when we get right with him.

# NOTES

1. You may want to explore the Mystery Religions that were strong at the time of Jesus, or the many religions that were rampant in those days. A good book on the subject is *The Early Church*, by Glen Hinson (Nashville: Abingdon, 1996).

2. First Corinthians 2:2, "For I resolved to know nothing while I was with you except Jesus *Christ* and *him crucified*" (NIV; emphasis added).

3. I think it would sidetrack the message to try to explain the councils and what they decided.

4. You can read more about being on the road to mission with Jesus in my book *Unfreezing Moves* (Nashville: Abingdon, 2001).

# CHAPTER 4

# LOOKING INWARD SO WE CAN TURN OUTWARD

### KEY IDEA

WHEN ATTEMPTING TO TURN AROUND A CHURCH OR TAKE A CHURCH TO ANOTHER LEVEL, YOU DO NOT WANT TO LOOK INWARD ANY LONGER THAN YOU HAVE TO TO DEVELOP A SOLID COMMUNITY OF FAITH. THE GOAL IS ALWAYS TO HAVE YOUR PEOPLE FOCUSED OUTWARD.

This chapter takes a bit of a departure from the constant outreach theme of the first few weeks of preaching. The focus of this message is on the need to reach inward and establish the core values of the church. Keep in mind that, by this time, I have spent several weeks focusing on the need of the church to reach out. I will also quickly return to the theme of outreach after one message on establishing the DNA of the mission, and I suggest that you do also. If your church already has good mission, vision, and values statements in place that are actually used to make day-to-day and major decisions, you may want to show how your vision fits into the DNA and how the congregation can remain outwardly focused or move further in that direction. Giving examples of past victories can help build the momentum and inspire people to move forward.

Depending on the situation, if the church doesn't have a mission statement, you may want to run a mission statement by the congregation. Or if the church has an acceptable mission statement, you may want to highlight it, take it at face value, and include it in your message. I've found when a church I'm consulting with has a good mission statement it helps to say, "I will take your mission statement seriously as I make recommendations at the end of the consultation." That would translate as, "While serving as your pastor, I'm going to take this mission statement seriously in my leadership."

If your church is a restart, simply say, "This is the mission of our church. Whoever wants to make it happen, join me." If your church is declining and doesn't have a mission statement, then just use the biblical mandate, which is "Our mission is to make disciples of Jesus Christ."

## Unity and Mission

Immediately after Jesus said that God's mission is like an ever-widening circle, reaching out to more and more people, the Holy Spirit was poured forth into the world, so that Peter's sermon resulted in thousands of people being welcomed into the Body of Christ (Acts 1 and 2). The same can happen today if we allow God to move in our lives.

At the outset of the story of the church, the multiplication of disciples is show-cased for all to see. Clearly, God is saying that the purpose of the church is to win the world to faith in God through Jesus Christ. All through Acts the story is clear—God wants the church to have explosive growth.

However, this growth is not only predicated on devotion and obedience to Jesus, it's also dependent on God's people being on the same page. "All who believed were together and had all things in common" (Acts 2:44).

For a church to be healthy enough to transform the community around it, much less reach out to the world, the following has to happen:

- The DNA must be in place.
- The church must be warm enough to act as an incubator for new Christians and church members who have developed into maturity.
- The congregation must be united.
- The church must be willing to repent of its sin in order to find the power of God.
- Accountability must be guaranteed if unity and power are to be present.

This chapter is meant to be one message only, and I suggest using the five points above as the message outline.

## THE DNA MUST BE IN PLACE

We begin our journey by getting our DNA in place.

What is DNA? DNA expresses who we are as a congregation. It describes our reason for existence. Of course, every church has the same DNA—"to make disciples." But like human DNA, the DNA of every congregation is different. For example: you can look at blood and tell if it comes from an ape or a human. But you can also look at that same blood and tell which human or ape it came from. The same is true for a congregation. Every congregation has the same generic DNA—"to make disciples." However, every congregation has an individual DNA which has to bear some semblance to making disciples.

In other words, any valid DNA must have an outward thrust. It's never acceptable for the DNA to be some form of "taking care of ourselves." The focus of any healthy DNA is on the non-believer, even when attention is being given to developing the inner life of the congregation. In order for the DNA to be biblical, the congregation has to be focused outwardly rather than inwardly.

I have a personal DNA. It's "to help every person I meet to be a missionary for Jesus Christ." This DNA includes both the generic and the personal DNA.

You can insert your own DNA here. If the church has a good mission statement, use it, and tell them you are going to take it seriously. If it has a bad mission statement, you may *not* want to use it at this point in the series, but talk about the need to establish one. If you are in a church plant or restart church, you may want to simply state the new mission statement for the church. If you need to formulate the DNA, take a look at my book *Unfreezing Moves,* pages 87-93.

## THE CHURCH MUST BE AN INCUBATOR OF FAITH

The church must get its act together inwardly so it can be a witness to the nonbeliever. Thus, the heart of this message is that Christians must grow and be united so that the church can be an incubator of faith for those who have not yet heard.

You might find it helpful to use the metaphor of the church as an incubator in which underdeveloped babies are placed in order to begin thriving. Churches are like incubators—they must be warm and welcoming to the nonbeliever and the unchurched so they can grow and begin thriving. Peter Scholtes's song hits the bull's eye —"They will know we are Christians by our love."

One of the major changes over the past two decades is the shift from "believing before belonging" to "belonging before believing." In the past, people were expected to believe before they were allowed to belong. That wasn't the case in the first three centuries after Christ. Membership in the Body of Christ took some four years. The first Christians had to know the people long enough to see if their lives exemplified their faith, and the only way to know them well was to spend time with them. The non-believer was allowed to take part in some aspects of the fellowship. They clearly belonged before they believed.

> The church is an incubator of faith for the nonbeliever.

The same is true today in a pagan society. Christians and skeptical unchurched people need to be accepted enough by the members to feel as if they belong before they are going to be willing to believe. They have to see actual Christianity in action to relieve their doubts and skepticism. (You do know that the average person in the West is skeptical and cynical regarding Christianity, don't you?)

One reason our church has declined over the years is because some of our people have been downright mean to visitors. Some have actually asked them to get out of their pew! Others have scowled at them because of the way they were dressed. I heard of one instance of a drunken man being forcefully removed from the church even though he wasn't disturbing anyone. That kind of behavior destroys any chance the church might have to be an incubator of faith. So the next time it happens, I want some of you to hold the person accountable!

For the church to be an incubator of faith, it must:

- have a clear, owned, and managed DNA[1]—that is, the leaders allow the mission statement to guide all their decisions;
- be united in its mission and hold one another accountable to that mission;
- refuse to allow the needs of any individual in the church to hold it back from reaching out to the world.

## THE CHURCH MUST HAVE UNITY
### (ACTS 2:42-47)

*They devoted themselves to the apostles' teaching and fellowship, to the breaking of bread and the prayers. Awe came upon everyone, because many won-*

*ders and signs were being done by the apostles. All who believed were together and had all things in common.* (Acts 2:42-44)

L ater, you will see that although this passage has been used to show the unity of the early church, it is also a testimony to the fact that the "sent" people didn't "go" into all the world. Instead, they hunkered down in Jerusalem and became ingrown. We will talk about this later, in another message. What you see in this text is that the early Gentile church, not the early Jewish church, took the message to the entire world. The Gentile church, begun in Antioch, was a much different form of church. Here are the comparisons. You may want to use them later, when you come to Acts 15.

The early Jewish church:

1. Was 100 percent Jewish or Jewish converts.
2. Continued to practice "the law."
3. Held its "main event" worship at the Temple.
4. Practiced its faith in daily life.
5. Shared a common purse, as described in Acts 4.
6. Was marked by signs and wonders.
7. Spent significant time together outside of Temple worship.
8. Got together in one another's homes.
9. Failed to follow Jesus' command to go into all the world. Instead, they hunkered down and went nowhere. Jerusalem became Rome, or worse, an extended "church building."

Whereas the early Gentile church:

1. Met primarily in homes. There were no church buildings until much later.
2. Did not worship in any way, shape, or form like we do.
3. Did not have Scriptures to rely on.
4. Practiced the faith, rather than studied the faith.
5. Took accountability seriously.
6. Shared the gospel through living their lives rather than by "inviting their friends" to church.

7. Lived the Christian life.

8. Did not gather en masse on any particular day for a "joint" worship service.

9. Had lots of problems.

10. Shared their possessions liberally.

11. Was lay led.

12. Was less interested in "right doctrine" and more interested in right behavior.

13. Reserved proclamation (what we call preaching) for the pagans.

The early church devoted itself to four things, and these four things held the church tightly together. They were devoted to the apostles' teachings, to fellowship, to Holy Communion, and to prayer.

We should do the same, because God wants our church to be united in its community and its message. It's the unity of the church that allows us to have such a powerful thrust into the community around us. When the church is united, the community knows it. When it isn't, the community knows it. A divided church has little to no power, because God wants the church united.

One of the most powerful aspects of the early church was the clarity and solidarity with which it moved forward. The people of the church literally had "all things in common." In our language today, we call this "DNA." They were clear about their mission, vision, and core values. (Of course, we all know that they really didn't have all things in common, as seen in chapters 4–5. But we will get to that later.)

This clarity didn't come out of a vacuum. As we have seen, it arose out of their common devotion and obedience to God in Jesus Christ. For authentic DNA to be discovered, those doing the discovering must be devoted and obedient to Jesus Christ. Otherwise, the process is flawed from the beginning. Any authentic devotion and obedience to Jesus Christ always results in a passion for those who have not yet heard and experienced what Jesus has to offer. People who don't care about discipleship haven't yet experienced the fullness of redemption and shouldn't be part of any DNA discovery process.[2]

We should all learn a lesson here. It is folly to put people into leadership just to pacify someone or to put people into leadership when they have an ax to grind with someone in the church or with the agreed-upon DNA. Leaders should have "all things in common."

Whatever method you use to develop and embed DNA, you must never allow people to forget that the primary reason they are doing this is to foster a church environment so rich and unified that it becomes an incubator of faith for the non-believer. We want non-believers to sense God's love for them just by being around Christians.

## A WILLINGNESS TO REPENT
### (ACTS 2:37-41)

Repentance often precedes unity. What most of us overlook in Peter's sermon is his call to repentance. Peter knew that God's people needed to repent of their feelings of superiority and entitlement. First-century Judaism was much like mainstream Christianity today. The church felt entitled to God's good pleasure and had little concern for the non-Hebrew. It felt it was chosen because it was special, rather than thinking it was special because it was chosen. Sound familiar?[3]

> We need to repent of our feelings of entitlement because we are members, and we need to learn to be servants, because we are redeemed.

We must never feel entitled to God or to membership in our church, nor can we afford to be unconcerned for the non-Christian. Therefore, some of us may need to repent of our feelings of entitlement and unconcern before we can begin to work on our DNA. We must get "right" with God and our neighbor before beginning to work on our DNA. Before we can experience the kind of growth God has in store for us, we need to get "right" with God. That means some of us need to repent of our selfish, ingrown ways. Some of us need the salvation that only Christ can offer.

If your people are conflicted, they need to repent from their selfishness, and we need to tell them that.

At this point, I became very clear with my congregation: the actions of some of the people prior to and after my arrival were downright heathen, and I could not tell from their actions whether or not they were even Christians. I singled out some of the behavior I had experienced during those first few months and called for those who were acting that way to repent or leave. It was dead silent that morning. Over the next few weeks, more people left than repented or gave their lives to Christ. But the transition was underway. The exodus would not be complete for four or five more months.

I hit the entitlement issue head-on. I wish I had hit it much harder than I did, because nothing ruins a church more than multiple strands of DNA. It would take me months to figure that one out, and in the early years it cost us a lot of wasted time. But as I said earlier, I didn't push the repentance button. I should have had an altar call early in my ministry. I would have had a better read on who was getting it and who wasn't.

So I cast a vision of a new DNA—a church where "everyone is a minister of Jesus Christ." If I were to cast a vision today, it would be "everyone is a missionary of Jesus Christ."

Don't be afraid of casting vision on your first Sunday. In fact, you should have cast it in the interview process or whatever method your tribe uses to place new pastors. But you should keep in mind that there is the biblical vision that never changes—God wants us to make disciples of all people—and then there is the more narrow vision that's born out of our own experiences. Just make sure that whatever vision you cast early on is born out of Scripture and God's claim on your life.

## THE CHURCH MUST HOLD ONE ANOTHER ACCOUNTABLE (ACTS 4–5)

The story of Ananias and Sapphira is simple but frightening. The church had decided that everyone would sell all their possessions and bring the money into the church. But one couple decided to hold back a piece of the price they received from selling some property. When confronted with what they had done, they lied and were struck dead. Their sin was not holding back some of the proceeds—we have evidence that others did the same. Their sin was saying they were giving their all when, in fact, they hadn't. They lied to the community. There can be no trust, no fellowship, when people are dishonest.

This chilling account of the sudden deaths of Ananias and Sapphira makes us face the fact that God deals with sin, especially church members' deceit and lack of integrity.

Now it doesn't matter how literally you interpret Scripture, the point is very clear—God expects honesty and unity within the local church. And when disunity rears its ugly head, God takes action and holds the guilty party accountable.

> # The story of Ananias and Sapphira sets forth the seriousness of accountability and unity within the Body.

This story wasn't just thrown in by the author. It sets forth two fundamental issues: the importance of accountability and unity within the Body. Unity doesn't happen if people aren't held accountable to some standard.

It's rare to see church leaders holding their flocks accountable for their sins, much less their unhealthy actions toward others in their church.

Because the early church had such a close community, any deviation from that unity was seen as a major threat to the mission. Any sign of deviation from the perceived truth was attacked with a vengeance. Many of Paul's letters to the churches were about disunity. Christians should hold one another accountable when they break the unity of the church. Healthy churches do not tolerate any form of disunity.

Most major problems in a church don't start out big. They were allowed to fester over time, until dysfunction became a characteristic of the church rather than an event. When people aren't held accountable for small things, they become major disruptors in the church.

## AN ACCOUNTABILITY STORY

I will never forget an experience I had with Wayne Cordeiro some ten years ago. I took a group of church planters to Honolulu to spend three days with Wayne (this was long before he became so well-known in the U.S.). The group was so impressed with the spirit within the church on Sunday morning that the first question they asked Wayne was, "How did this church come to have such a wonderful spirit?" Wayne's answer floored them. As is his custom, he answered them with a story.

"Late one night when we were setting up for worship, one of the men snapped at one of the women. He didn't curse her; he just snapped angrily at her. So I took him aside and told him that kind of spirit wasn't welcomed here and that he should go home until he got his spirit together."

The group didn't know what to say, other than, "You sent him home for something that small?" To which Wayne replied, "Jesus said, 'You have been faithful over a few things; I will make you ruler over many.' Small problems become big problems if not held accountable when small."

Think about how it would change our church if every member was held accountable for his or her actions? Can you imagine the grief that might be eliminated today, if in the past, the light of the gospel had been shined on conflicted people before they became dysfunctional? They might have been changed.

How much more of an incubator of faith could our church become if we held every leader accountable?

## ACTS 6:1-7

*The Hellenists complained against the Hebrews because their widows were being neglected in the daily distribution of food. And the twelve called together the whole community of the disciples and said, "It is not right that we should neglect the word of God in order to wait on tables. Therefore, friends, select from among yourselves seven men of good standing, full of the Spirit and of wisdom, whom we may appoint to this task, while we, for our part, will devote ourselves to prayer and to serving the word."... They chose Stephen, a man full of faith and the Holy Spirit.... The word of God continued to spread; the number of the disciples increased greatly in Jerusalem.*

This is a pivotal text in the life of the early church. Like so many entitled church members today, those early Christians wanted their pastors to take care of them, rather than transform the city. They wanted their pastors to be little more than "hit men" who were expected to do the entire ministry on behalf of the entitled members. The above Scripture speaks to that heresy. If we want to be a church that transforms our city, we must not make that mistake.

I can't help you grow this church if you require me to spend most of my time in hospitals and rest homes. Still, these folks are part of the church and need ministering to. This is where texts on the priesthood of the believer and Ephesians 4:11-12 come into play (you may want to quote Ephesians 4:11-12). If our church is to grow, it's imperative that you not expect me to do the entire ministry. The every-day ministry is part of what the church is encouraged to do by Paul when he says we are to "bear one another's burdens" (Gal. 6:2).

There's a lot of difference between taking care of people and transforming them. We can take care of people without transforming them, but we can't trans-form them without taking care of them. The twelve were right—the duty of the lead-ers is never to care for one another, but to see to it that everyone is cared for. Why? So the church will be loving enough that it's an incubator for those who have not experienced Jesus.

A t this point, even though I don't like talking about "lay" ministry, I use this passage as the justification for lay ministries.

The earliest church came really close to turning inward. But, thank God, as time and events unfolded, it did not—and we must not.

A s you prepare to preach any message, keep in mind that the most outwardly facing church is just one decision away from turning in-ward! So gather the DNA, but don't let the church become comfortable focusing in on itself.

## TAKING IT HOME

If we're going to reach out and transform this city, you're going to have to allow me to spend more time in the community than in the office, in the hospitals, and in members' homes. You're going to have to allow me to function biblically and equip you to care for one another and to reach out with me to the city. We must not turn inward, or else we will die, and our city will never experience the transformation it needs.

# NOTES

1. "Owned and managed" means the mission, vision, and values drive every decision made by your church, and the leaders can recite the mission statement from memory.

2. For a quick and effective method of discovering DNA in a church free of major conflict and controllers, see my book *Unfreezing Moves*, pp. 92-93.

3. You can find a repentance graphic on the support page.

CHAPTER 5

# MULTIPLYING THE MOVEMENT

## KEY IDEA

FAST, EXPLOSIVE GROWTH IS BIBLICAL. GOD EXPECTS OUR
CHURCH AND THE KINGDOM TO GROW AND GROW AND GROW!

We must now get back to the major theme of my first six months—God wants the church to reach out to the unchurched. You can't speak about this theme enough because, left to its own, the church will always return to focusing on itself. That's simply part of our basic sin and one reason spiritual leaders are needed.

This could be a challenging series of messages. If your church is declining, there will be lots of push-back on the part of the leaders. They will protest that significantly growing the church isn't biblical, much less possible for their church. If your church is growing, it may be time to think about planting a church or going multi-site.[1] Either way, you'll have a challenge.

### Biblical Growth

In these messages I wanted the congregation to know that God expects fast, explosive growth of the Kingdom and the church. You can build upon this text and show how, throughout Acts, God shows us that fast, explosive growth of the Kingdom and the church is biblical. For instance:

Acts 1 and 2 tell us that the early church went from 120 believers to 3,120 believers overnight. Then Acts 2:47 tells us that "day by day the Lord added to their number those who were being saved." The number of Christians was growing daily! Acts 4:4 says that many of the people who heard their message believed, and the number of believers totaled about 5,000 men, not counting women and children.

> # Fast, explosive growth is biblical. God expects your church and the Kingdom to grow!

But then Acts 6:1 says, "The believers rapidly multiplied" (NLT). It is only now that the writer uses the word *rapidly*. So from zero to twenty thousand, Luke didn't consider the growth to be rapid.

But this wildfire growth wasn't over. Acts 21 uses another word to describe the growth—*myriads*. That means tens of thousands of believers now in Jerusalem. The number of believers at this point in the story is staggering. The church in Jerusalem reached what Malcolm Gladwell calls the "tipping point."[2] Over the next five centuries, Christianity would spread so rapidly that it claimed the allegiance of the majority of the Roman Empire.[3] This was crazy, psycho growth. And that's what God wants to happen in your church. Can you visualize it?

A movement was underway that was spreading across the continent. Everywhere Christians went, they spread the good news. That's the blueprint God wants for our church.

> Keep in mind that this was a bankrupt church ready to close and, because of my first few weeks of preaching, was actually dwindling in size.[4]

What's keeping you from asking God to multiply our ministry? Right now, would you just ask God to explode the dream you have? Would you ask God to help us reach the entire city?

> I remember one service during this series where I asked the congregation to get down on their knees and ask God to give them a message of hope for the city. I said to them, "We're not just going to build a church; we're going to change a city." I lost some members over that—who was I to ask them to get down on their knees?
>
> Remember to continue to drive home the point that the growth of their church is not what's at stake. It's the growth of the Kingdom.

How are we going to evaluate the success of our church—by membership, stable finances, baptisms, or worship attendance? The Scriptures don't justify any of these methods of evaluation. Instead, God evaluates the success of the mission by how much of the city the church reaches with the good news. It's not how big the church is; the issue is how many of the people in our city we have reached for Christ. Remember the Ever-widening Circle? That's what God wants here. The transformation of the city and the world is what God is about, not the growth of our church. However, if we transform the city for Christ, our church will grow, as well as the other churches in town.

A
t this point, the people of my church began to gather into two camps—those who thought I was crazy and those whose eyes began to light up. As the weeks went by, it became easier and easier to tell the difference between those who got it and those who would never get it.

What are you doing in your preaching that is causing people to wonder about your sanity? Are you willing to ask them to join you in a quest to transform your city? Or are you hung up on the numbers? If so, you will never grow a faithful, biblical church. Growth is biblical.

## Biblical growth requires deep commitment, reaching out to the unchurched, and personal conversion.

So how can we begin a movement that will transform the city? Where do we start? This kind of growth is dependent on three things:

- deep commitment
- reaching out to the unchurched
- personal conversion

Let's take a look at the three requirements for fast, multiplying, Kingdom growth.

### Acts 7–8

*While they were stoning Stephen, he prayed, "Lord Jesus, receive my spirit." Then he knelt down and cried out in a loud voice, "Lord, do not hold this sin against them." When he had said this, he died.*

*And Saul approved of their killing him.*

*That day a severe persecution began against the church in Jerusalem, and all except the apostles were scattered throughout the countryside of Judea and Samaria. Devout men buried Stephen and made loud lamentation over him. But Saul was ravaging the church by entering house after house; dragging off both men and women, he committed them to prison.* (Acts 7:59–8:3)

## TRANSFORMING A CITY REQUIRES GOD'S PEOPLE TO BE DEEPLY COMMITTED TO THE MISSION

Stephen's preaching and Christ-like example were so powerful and convicting that they got him stoned to death.[5] He became the first Christian martyr on record. He took his commitment seriously, and it cost him all that he had. He wasn't playing church, and neither should we.

Stephen was stoned to death, and then Saul began his rampage against the church. This was not a good time to be committed to Christ, but that is what such growth demands—deep, personal commitment—even a willingness to suffer for the cause of Christ. Are we up to it? Are we willing to do without in order to see this mission through and do our part in increasing the Ever-widening Circle?

You may want to use Matthew 23:36-38, where Jesus shows his compassion for the city of Jerusalem. If you do, it's important for you to convey Jesus' compassion for the city and ask your people to join you in praying for the transformation of your city. You may even want to take your small group out one night to some place where you can overlook the city—a restaurant, a hill, or tall building—and literally pray for the city.

Growing our church to the point that it could actually have part in transforming the city will take more commitment than I see among us at the moment. We need to make a commitment to this city, rather than to our church or denomination. We must step up to another level of commitment and take the four vows of our denomination seriously—"I will support my church with my prayers, presence, gifts, and service (there is a fifth one now—witness)." Everyone who joins this church from now on and anyone in leadership will be held accountable to those vows, even if it costs me my job.

N ow remember—I was restarting a church, so I could do things you might not be able to do right away or as bluntly as I did. You must weigh the context and see how far and how fast you can proceed to your goal.

Now, just so you don't miss it—the stoning of Stephen led to a wholesale persecution that resulted in most of the Christians being driven out of Jerusalem into the "ends of the earth." In a strange way, the stoning of Stephen resulted in a positive—God's people were forced to leave Jerusalem and take the gospel to the "ends of the earth." The Acts 1:8 church was beginning to materialize.

### Acts 8

*Now those who were scattered went from place to place, proclaiming the word. Philip went down to the city of Samaria and proclaimed the Messiah to them.* (Acts 8:4-5)

Philip was one of the Christians who fled Jerusalem to Samaria. He is also the first person on record to reach out to the least, the last, and the lost. He connected with the people most hated by the Jews—Samaritans. But even though Philip had a thriving ministry in Samaria, God called him to leave and go to what many considered the "ends of the earth"—Ethiopia. First-century Romans or Greeks believed Ethiopians lived literally at the southern edge of the earth.

> Transforming the city also requires an intense desire to reach out to those who have not yet responded to the good news.

Philip led the Ethiopian to Christ and then went wandering through the countryside proclaiming Jesus. Philip was part of the actual fulfillment of Jesus' last words—"Go make disciples of all nations" (Matt. 28:18). The gospel was going full-circle and in such a short time. Philip's response to the Ethiopian is proof that God was actively fulfilling his purposes for the scope of the church's mission. Philip's excitement was off the chart!

But that's the way it is with all Christians when they lead someone to Christ. When was the last time you led someone to Christ? You don't know what you're missing. I challenge you to begin making relationships with people who don't believe and, in time, to bring them to church.

> This is also a good time to begin a small group where you are going to raise up a band of evangelists, if you haven't already done so.

The conversion of the Ethiopian eunuch graphically demonstrates the inclusiveness of the gospel and foreshadows what was to come over the next five centuries. No apparent obstacle—whether physical defect, race, or geographical remoteness—can place a person beyond the saving call of the good news. What prejudices are getting in the way of your talking with your neighbor about Jesus? What fears are holding you back? I'd be glad to talk with you one-on-one if you're open to it. Just call me.

### Acts 9

*Meanwhile Saul, still breathing threats and murder against the disciples of the Lord, went to the high priest and asked him for letters to the synagogues at Damascus, so that if he found any who belonged to the Way, men or women, he might bring them bound to Jerusalem. Now as he was going along and approaching Damascus, suddenly a light from heaven flashed around him. He fell to the ground and heard a voice saying to him, "Saul, Saul, why do you persecute me?" He asked, "Who are you, Lord?" The reply came, "I am Jesus, whom you are persecuting. But get up and enter the city, and you will be told what you are to do." (Acts 9:1-6)*

Most of us know something about the Apostle Paul. But how much do we know about Paul before his conversion? His name before his conversion was Saul. And Saul was on a rampage. He was doing everything he could to stamp out Christianity before it got a foothold.

> The transformation of the city requires a personal conversion of those who will lead the charge.

Saul was on his way to Damascus to arrest as many Christians as he could find. Then Saul met Jesus, and nothing was ever again the same, not even his name. Now Saul became known as Paul. His name was changed because he was no longer the same person. He was made new in Christ.

You see—when we meet Christ, everything about us changes. We are a new creature in Christ. This experience so transformed Saul that later Paul would write the following words to the church at Corinth: "Therefore if anyone is in Christ, he is a new creature; the old things passed away; behold, new things have come" (2 Cor. 5:17 NASB). My hope for you is that you are a new creature in Christ. If not, let's talk about it after the service.

Later, we will learn from Paul himself that one thing that drove his vendetta against Christianity was his pride. He was proud of his tradition, and Christianity threatened it. He was proud to be a Hebrew (Phil. 3:4-5); proud to be a Pharisee and the son of a Pharisee (Acts 23:6). We know that pride goes before a fall, but are you aware that pride usually gets in the way of conversion? Do you know that conversion destroys whatever pride stands in the way of obedience and devotion to Jesus Christ?

The same can be true with us. Our pride can get in our way of following Jesus. We like the way our church is at the moment. We like the power and control we have over what does and does not happen in our church. We don't want to submit to the Lordship of Jesus Christ. But we must. We have no choice if we are Christians. So many times it comes down to this—are we Christians or church members? There is a world of difference. If you don't know the difference, let's talk about it after the service.

How do we know Paul's conversion was for real? How do we know our conversion is for real? By watching what happens as a result of conversion. Paul immediately began sharing his faith and performing marvelous acts among the people. So much so that people were astonished at what he was doing. They couldn't believe he was the same person. But Paul kept them baffled, the Scripture says, "by proving that Jesus is the Christ" (Acts 9:22 NIV). And how did he prove Jesus was the Christ? By how he lived before them.

After our conversions, did the world look upon us differently because of who we were and what we've become?

Of course, if your church practices infant baptism you may have to re-word this.

You see, the way to tell if a person really is a Christian is by watching how he or she lives. Do you have a life worth watching?[6] Do you realize that you are the curriculum? How you live just might determine what another person does with Jesus.[7]

The conversion of Saul is such an important event in the history of the growth of the church, there are three versions of the conversion story, all showing different aspects of conversion (Acts 9, 22, 26). Also, Paul shares his conversion story over and over throughout his writings. Our conversion is the central piece of our life with God. It is what we are becoming, and as such, we should be able to tell our own story when the opportunity arises.

> I don't think it is helpful to discuss what the differences in the versions are, but it is helpful to point out how important both Luke and Paul considered the event to be.
>
> I would emphasize that most people today do not come to faith the way Saul did because we have entered a post-modern world where most non-churched people are skeptical of religion. So more conversions happen over an extended time, much like a process, rather than the dramatic kind Paul had.

Anger is much easier to work through than skepticism. The kind of hatred Saul had for Christians is easier to convert than skepticism. Skepticism is one of the harder nuts for evangelism to crack. That is why it is essential for us to form friendships outside the church and why conversion today is more of a process than in Paul's day. Conversion today is almost always preceded by some form of extended friendship.

In the emerging world, effective evangelism relies on long-term relationships and growth processes—not rallies, laws, or programs. It's not unusual for individuals to take two to four years to realize that they have committed their lives to God through Christ.

## TAKING IT HOME

So what about it? Have you given your life to Christ? Are you in the process of turning your life over to Christ? Or are you committed enough to Christ to be part of the transformation of our city and the multiplication of the kingdom of God? Either way, you're welcome to join us on our journey.

# NOTES

1. For more information on church planting and multi-site churches go to http://church-consultations.com/plantingmultisite/.

2. Malcolm Gladwell, *The Tipping Point* (Boston: Little, Brown and Company, 2000).

3. Kenneth LaTourette, *A History of Christianity*, Vol. 1 (New York: HarperCollins, 1975), p. 65.

4. If you want more information about what makes a movement successful, see my book *Unfreezing Moves*, chapter 1.

5. See the support page for a large graphic about the stoning of Stephen.

6. To read the chapter "A Life Worth Watching," see my book *A Second Resurrection* (Nashville: Abingdon, 2007).

7. For two articles about "You Are the Curriculum," go to the support page.

# CHAPTER 6

# SHARING YOUR STORY

---

### KEY IDEA

CHRISTIANS MUST DEVELOP RELATIONSHIPS WITH
PEOPLE OUTSIDE OF THEIR CHURCH.

---

I really didn't like Doug. He was rough, his language was foul, and sometimes he smelled. But he played a good game of golf, and golfers of my caliber were hard to find in seminary. So I *sort of* befriended him.

One day, he asked me why I went to seminary. He actually opened the door for me, but I didn't want to walk through it and share my story. We had been playing golf together for a couple of months. That was our only relationship. Other than that, I didn't even like him. But for some reason, he not only liked me, he trusted me. So my conscience got the best of me, and in the nineteenth hole, I shared Christ with him. And guess what? He was ready to hear, and he accepted Christ. I felt elated but also ashamed. Why did it take me so long to walk through the door he had opened for me—because my faith was weak?

Ever had such an experience? Surely you have. If so, begin this message with your story and tell the congregation how you felt. If you were like me, let them see you squirm as well as experience your joy in the end. If you eagerly jumped in the conversation, let them see your eagerness to share your faith. If you have never led a person to Christ, you shouldn't preach this message. Instead, I encourage you to ask God to send someone your way so you can share your faith with them and then describe to the congregation how this is a first for you and how you felt doing it, and then invite them to do the same.

You see, most people never share their faith with anyone. Studies show it takes 85 people to win one person to Christ every year. Think about it—85 people to make one disciple. Which group are you in—the 85 who never lead someone to Christ or the 15 who do? Which group would you prefer to be a part of? Better yet, which group do you think God wants you in?

The problem is that most of us don't feel bad about being part of the 85. So I'm hoping some of us will have our consciences pricked today and will begin to seek out ways to share our faith. As your Christian friends see you struggle with this issue, some of them will gain the courage to share their faith as well. And the movement will begin—because you dared to share your faith with a friend.

The problem with most churches is that they have so many committees and programs that, by the time their members finish their obligations to the institutional church, they don't have any time to develop friendships outside of the church. It is commonly accepted that once a person has been a Christian for more than three years, the odds are he or she doesn't have any solid relationships with nonchurched people, much less nonbelievers. That's one reason we need to streamline our church and do away with as many committees as possible—so people have time to spend with nonchurched people outside of these four walls. That's why I'm suggesting eliminating the worship and evangelism committees. We don't need them, and they get in the way.

## Acts 10

The story of Peter and Cornelius is a priceless look at how people react to sharing their faith and the role God plays in evangelism. It's also a great picture of the reluctance of people to engage in sharing their faith and the surprise they have when they find out that most of the work of redemption is already done before they open their mouths.

Cornelius was a soldier and a Gentile who had a dream in which he was told a man named Peter would be visiting him. At the same time, Peter had a dream in which God asked him to go eat pork with a Gentile! Now, a Jew couldn't be asked to do anything worse than eat pork with a Gentile. God was asking Peter to break a Jewish law which forbad a Jew from associating with a Gentile, much less sit down to dinner with one. Can't you just imagine the horror Peter must have felt? God was calling into question one of the basic tenets of Peter's Jewish faith. Nothing could be more sacrilegious than to sit down with a Gentile and eat pork. Doing so broke dozens of Jewish laws.

Y ou may feel the need here to explain the Jewish law about eating any animals with cloven hooves—I didn't.

Peter didn't want to go eat pork with a Gentile. It was degrading to him and his faith. But if he was going to be a major player in taking the gospel to the "ends of the earth," God had to move him out of his comfort zone, just like he has to move us out of our comfort zone if we want to transform our city.

> Will we wrestle with the need to turn totally outward and spend more time, energy, and money on reaching the lost than we spend on ourselves?

But the interesting thing about this text is that, when Peter finally agreed to go, he found that God had already softened Cornelius's heart. As a result of Peter's visit, not just Cornelius but other Gentiles also became Christians.

Now, this should bring some comfort to those of us who are not sure about sharing our faith with our friends. We aren't alone in this journey. Like Peter, we realize that when we go out into the world, God is already there, preparing their hearts to receive our message. We should take comfort that most nonbelievers have had contact with God before we ever enter their lives. We should learn to look for those experiences and build on them, like Peter did with Cornelius. Remember the promise of the Holy Spirit we read about in Acts 2? The Spirit will go before us, preparing our way.

Our city is filled with people like Cornelius. God has prepared them for us to share with them the good news. All they need is for us to walk across the room or yard or street to them. That's all that's lacking!

And let's not overlook the fact that God is also telling us in this story that he can make the unclean clean. The story isn't just about eating pork with a Jew, although that's a central part of the story. It's also a reminder that none of us need to remain unclean because God makes the unclean clean—even those whom we don't like.

One more thing about this story: both Peter and Cornelius had a vision from God. Christians sometimes think they are the only ones who hear God. We aren't. God can speak to anyone.

Spend at least one message on this text. If you have lots of experiences to share, develop them into two or three messages.

Two things about this story stand out: one, even the strongest of Christians finds it hard to leave the comfort of their church to go out and share their faith with someone they don't even know. Two, it helps to know that God will always go ahead of us and prepare the heart of the person with whom we are going to share our faith. (There is a sense in which God already resides in every person due to God's part in creation.)

## Relational Evangelism

I made sure the congregation understood that I was not talking about cold turkey, in-your-face evangelism. They need to hear this from you up-front.

One year while I was still pastor of Colonial Hills, my worship team and I did a short workshop tour. At one stop our drummer got sick, and we needed a replacement. The only replacement we could find, a non-Christian, rehearsed with the group each evening before the workshops. On the third evening, he said to the group, "This has been a wonderful experience. I don't know what you folks have, but I want it. I don't think I will ever be the same again. Tell me more about Jesus." I don't know whatever happened to this guy, but my guess is that night, he began the journey of faith.

Another way to describe it is that we are moving from "being saved" to "being transformed." Being transformed differs from being saved. Being saved suggests more of an event; whereas, being transformed suggests a long-term process through a variety of events. Involvement in the mission out of which one is transformed is often the end result of being transformed ourselves. Often, it is hard to separate one's transformation from one's mission. Behavior and belief merge.

> # Christians are called to do things that make us feel uncomfortable. So get over it!

Membership in a church isn't our goal. In many cases, the only purpose for encouraging membership is to be able to hold key leaders to a much higher standard of behavior than before.[1] If church membership is all you're getting out of coming here, then you're wasting your time. God wants you, not your membership.

Evangelism today is about establishing relationships with our networks—waiting until people are ready for us to share our faith, and if they are never ready, then at least we have a new friend.

But if we spend time nurturing a relationship with our neighbor, it's not unlikely that our faith will begin to prepare their hearts, even if we haven't said a word about our faith. Our life says more than we know. Just by being around us, they should begin to consider Jesus.

Often, this is the case with relational evangelism. If we have gotten to know the person well and have become a part of his or her life, we begin to feel the rhythm of his or her life. We develop a sixth sense as to when to share our faith. Often, the friend opens the door the same way Cornelius did with Peter or Doug did with me that day on the golf course.

> I told them stories about how I used to be able to share the faith with people I hardly knew and lead them to Christ. But today, that's very rare because the world has changed (but don't get sidetracked on how the world has changed). Today, because people are more skeptical about religion, it takes much longer. We have to establish relationships with nonbelievers. As Willow Creek Community Church Pastor Bill Hybels often says, "People don't care how much you know until they know how much you care."

That's one of the reasons I would rather you be involved in some secular activity than sitting on a church committee or board. People who spend all of their time at church lose most of their non-churched relationships. When that happens, the church is in trouble.

Should you wish to teach some on how to share faith without being a bigot, the following might help (you might want to share this at a board meeting or leadership team meeting):

Begin where they are, not where you are or where you would like them to be. Remember, it's not about *you*; it's about them and their relationship with God. You must first care about *their* story before you can share *your* story on the way to *the* story. Of course, this takes time. You have to first develop a real relationship, one that isn't built around bait and switch. So never try to be someone you're not. Develop real relationships, and if your friends ever open the door, share your faith with them.

The Socratic method of asking questions is often the most effective method of communication. Ask questions about them. Never begin with "the Bible says" because that is deadly in today's world. For a list of sample questions to ask, go to the support page.

## CHRISTIANS ARE CALLED TO DO THINGS THAT MAY FEEL UNCOMFORTABLE

Up until this time, no one other than Jews and Samaritans had been baptized into the Christian faith. Cornelius, however, was what the Scriptures called a "God-fearer." He didn't fit any of the previous molds. "God-fearers" had adopted the Jewish faith with their code of morality and attended synagogue services but were not full converts and did not want to submit to circumcision. They were regarded as outside the fellowship of Jewish communities. Even though many Gentiles had adopted some of the tenets of Judaism, none had converted to Christianity, so Cornelius's experience is a watershed moment. The gospel had broken out of the Jewish circle and, as we saw in a previous message, the way was prepared for the gospel to spread to the edge of the known world.

The fact that Peter didn't want to go to Cornelius is so powerful when we understand the dynamics. God was asking Peter to do something so distasteful to a Jew that it would make most Jews throw up. "You want me to do what, God? Surely you're not asking me to eat pork with a Gentile! My God, Jews don't do that! Jews don't eat pork, and certainly not with Gentiles."

If Peter had trouble sharing his faith with someone different from him, it's no wonder we struggle with it. The question before us is, "Will we wrestle with the need to turn totally outward and spend more time, energy, and money on reaching the lost than we spend on ourselves?" That's the question I want each of you in the congregation to wrestle with over the next few months.

replayed that theme over and over throughout my preaching from Acts.

Many times, God calls us to do things we don't want to do or aren't comfortable doing. It's up to us not to question, but to do. Growing a church and the Kingdom always causes problems and challenges.

So why do we want to grow this church? Because that is what we were put here to do—it's not an option. So over the next few months, all of us will be called upon to do some things we're not used to doing; some things that we may not want to do; some things that will cause us discomfort; but all of these things will be only at the prompting of the Holy Spirit and in the name of growing this church forward and transforming our city.

Whether we like it or not, God calls every authentic leader into the world, to be with people who make us uncomfortable. If we spend all of our time with people we like and are comfortable with, we are failing in our God-given responsibilities.

> God often asks us to do the very thing that challenges us the most.

Life is full of things none of us like to do but are beneficial to our personal growth in the long run. Because God knows our hearts God often asks us to do the very thing that challenges us the most. God looks into our hearts and asks us to do the very thing we most don't want to do because God knows that, in doing so, we will grow.

Few of us enjoy exercise, but without it, we grow old prematurely. And what about saving for the future when you badly want to spend the money on something today?

I can't remember all of the examples I used, but you get the point. I'm sure you have some things in your life that you don't enjoy doing but that pay great dividends over the long haul. Share those things with your congregation.

You're going to get some push-back on this message. "Pastor, surely you're not asking me to talk to my neighbor about Jesus. Get real." But that is exactly what you want to ask them to do over the next few months. Tell them you will do it with them. Let them know you have the same fears they do, and if you've overcome the fear of sharing your faith, tell them how you did it. If not, share your journey with them over the next few months. When people actually share their faith, let some of them give their testimony during worship. It will encourage others to do the same.

I doubt if most of the people in your congregation want to become involved enough with their neighbors that they can invite them to church, much less to your small group, or even more, to share their faith with them. Every study shows that sharing one's faith is one of the hardest aspects of being a Christian.

There isn't any one way to share your faith. Jesus responded differently to people based on what he felt they needed—the rich, young ruler; the blind man; Nicodemus; and Zacchaeus are some examples.

You may want to spend time on each of these, and you can find more examples based on what you know about your church.

In other words, there isn't any one way to share your faith with another person. The key is to learn what comes naturally to you.

Find your own ways to milk this section, because most of your people are either afraid to share their faith or have some form of arrogance toward those around them.

### FEAR IS NORMAL

I shared with them the first time I shared my faith with someone. I related to them how nervous I was. I recounted the many times I visited newcomers to the church and prayed as I knocked on the door, "Lord, don't let them be home!" You may have some folks in your church who have overcome such fear. If so, ask them to give a testimony about how they overcame it and how overcoming it changed their lives.

During the first six months of this series, I took a group of people with me every Saturday to hang door-knockers and to ask the people who were home a very pointed question about what they needed from the church. Several of them had some very good conversations at the doors of people we visited and later were gratified to see some of them actually showing up in worship. I had them tell their experiences.

Let's get real for a moment. All of us are afraid to witness at times. It's natural—we're invading people's most private moments. In some cases, we're intruders of the worst kind. In other cases, we're mere nuisances. However, our fears should be lessened by knowing that God will go before us and help us and give us the right words to say. Listen to what Jesus told his disciples: "And I tell you, everyone who acknowledges me before others, the Son of Man also will acknowledge before the angels of God; but whoever denies me before others will be denied before the angels of God. . . . When they bring you before the synagogues, the rulers, and the authorities, do not worry about how you are to defend yourselves or what you are to say; for the Holy Spirit will teach you at that very hour what you ought to say" (Luke 12:8-9, 11-12).

When we share our faith with others, we should learn to rely more on God than on ourselves. So the more we prepare our hearts with God's word and the closer we are to God, the more likely we are to say the right thing at the right moment. Now, do you see why I said a few weeks ago that obedience and devotion to Jesus are the foundations on which you need to build your faith? It's not about us; it's about God.

One key thing we need to remember—in the absence of a deep love for Christ, fear fills the gap. Remember, "There is no fear in love, but perfect love casts out fear" (1 John 4:18). This presence of fear is why it is so important to be involved in weekly devotionals. If we allow our faith to weaken, fear fills the void, and we find ourselves fearful of anything that's beyond what we deem to be possible. Remember, God is not found in the possible. God is found more profoundly in the impossible. So if you feel it is impossible to share your faith, then you are closer to God than you may want to admit.[2]

## SHARING FAITH IS THE ESSENCE OF THE CHURCH

Even though not everyone is called or gifted to share their faith, we still have to remember that every church is expected to share Jesus Christ with the world. That is what the church exists to do. No exceptions exist. Churches don't have the luxury of putting themselves at the center of their ministry. Everyone is expected to support the effort by their church to reach out and share Jesus Christ. Sharing our faith is the essence of the church. Not programs, not quilting, not anything but sharing Jesus.

This essence goes all the way back to God's blessing of Abraham. God blessed Abraham because Abraham was willing to submit to God's authority. But the key to this passage is why God blessed Abraham. The object of God's blessing wasn't Abraham; the objects were those who would come after Abraham and be blessed because of what Abraham began. "Now the LORD said to Abram, 'Go from your country and your kindred and your father's house to the land that I will show you. I will make of you a great nation, and I will bless you, and make your name great, so that you will be a blessing'" (Gen. 12:1-2).

The church has been blessed and set apart by God for the specific purpose of being a blessing to those around it—"blessed to be a blessing." As Abraham was chosen by God and sent out on his journey to father a great nation that would be a blessing to all, so the church is chosen, not because we are special. We are special because we are chosen to be a blessing to the world.

So let's just clear the air—if a church is so ingrown and self-absorbed that it acts more like a hospice or a hospital than the church, it's not a church. We don't want that to happen to us—do we? I know I don't and won't be a part of that kind of church—ever.

## WE CAN RESIST AND BE UNFULFILLED OR RESPOND
## AND FIND FULFILLMENT

The nightmare God kept sending to Peter finally wore him down. Peter gave up and went to Cornelius.

I want you to know—God isn't going to give up on us, so we might as well go and be part of this church's witness to the city.

God bugged Peter over and over, and God won't let us rest either. We might as well give up also and begin developing relationships with non-Christians or unchurched people.

So what's keeping you from sharing your faith with those you know so well you know your message would be well-received? Are you afraid? Do you not believe it deeply enough? Do you feel as if it would be invading someone's space? Listen carefully. If God opens a door for you to share your faith, you should walk through it, no matter how it makes you feel.

> If you have someone in your church who recently shared his or her faith with a friend, ask the person if he or she would close your message by sharing with the congregation how it felt to share their faith, especially if the friend responded by receiving Christ. If you don't have anyone to ask and you have led someone to Christ in the past, share with the congregation how you felt after doing so.

### CORNELIUS WAS READY

*Be strong and bold; have no fear . . . because it is the LORD your God who goes with you; he will not fail you or forsake you.* (Deut. 31:6)

When Peter got to Cornelius, he found that God was already at work. Believe it or not, Cornelius was reading scripture. All Peter had to do was confirm what Cornelius was experiencing. Often, that is the case after you spend time with your neighbor. They have seen the Christ within you, and it has rubbed off on them. All they need is for you to walk through the door and offer them Christ.

The sad thing is that most of our fears never materialize. It's rare for someone to hit, bite, or gore people for sharing their faith, especially among friends. Still, our fears paralyze us just the same.

The last thing we can afford to have happen in this church is for it to become so inwardly focused that we die as a church because God abandons us. Remember the text in Revelation—"But I have this against you, that you have abandoned the love you had at first" (Rev. 2:4).

Yes, it's true—like Elvis, God leaves the building when his people bottle up the good news and try to keep it to themselves. This church has made that mistake in the past. We dare not make that mistake again.

You may want to talk about God removing the candlestick from the church. It depends on how stuck the church is and how much leverage you think you have to put on them to get them to see the light. Of course, the more leverage you apply, the more push-back you will get. So you have to weigh the good with the bad here.

## THE GOOD NEWS

However we may feel about being a witness for Jesus, God expects it of us. We have little choice if we want to be faithful. Remember Acts 1:8, which included the words, "*be my witnesses.*" The word *witness* translates the word "martyr." The very last thing Jesus asked of us was that we be a witness to him.

However, the good news is that there are many ways to be a witness. Not everyone is gifted at verbally sharing their faith. That's why our church provides many avenues for people to become involved in evangelism.

- Open your home for a small group.
- Help with the guest sign-in on Sunday morning, so that timely responses can be made.
- Staff the information or response booth.
- Pray for the mission to transform the city.
- Be parking lot attendants who have smiles on your faces.
- Stand in the gap between pastor and layperson when opposition to the costs of transforming the city arises.

What other ways can you think of?

I'm sure your church offers some other avenues in which people can share in the outreach of your church. Show them the ways. You will do well in the closing to encourage your people to pray about signing up for one of the many ways they can become involved in evangelism through your church. I would list those opportunities in the worship folder and call their attention to them. I would also set aside time for them to pray about their involvement.

Warning: You want to be careful here not to give people with a gift for evangelism an out so they don't respond to God's call in their lives. You want people to see that many ways to be a witness exist, but you don't want to wind up with no verbal evangelists actively engaging their networks. So you walk a tightrope on this point.

## TAKING IT HOME

We couldn't close without referring to the fact that Cornelius had gathered his friends together to hear what Peter had to say. He wanted others to be blessed by Peter's ministry. And we should do the same. If our hearts overflow with God's love in Christ, it is only natural that we want to share it with others.

One of my favorite sayings is—"Life comes to us on its way to someone else. If we pass it on, we grow strong; if we keep it to ourselves, we wither and die."

Life is good when it is passed on; life sours when we keep it to ourselves.

You may want to close this message (or messages) by asking your people to pray for a moment and ask God to give them the names of two people to pray for over the next four weeks and to invite to their small group or Sunday school class or to some mission project like Habitat for Humanity (something nonthreatening). Take three to five minutes for this. Give your people enough time to take this invitation seriously. Then, ask them to write down these names on the place set aside in the worship folder, tear it off, and take it home to put it somewhere visible enough they won't be able to ignore it.

If you need more resources you might want to go to www.hitchhikers guidetoevangelism.com. There, you will find a load of helpful tools to get your people engaged with evangelism.

# NOTES

1. For an article on twenty-first-century evangelism, go to the support page.
2. For an article about the culture of fear, go to the support page.

CHAPTER 7

# BACKYARD MISSIONARIES

## KEY IDEAS

1. THIS IS THE POINT IN OUR STORY WHERE GOD INTENTIONALLY MAKES IT CLEAR THAT CHRIST IS FOR THE ENTIRE WORLD, NOT JUST THE JEWS.
2. IF WE'RE GOING TO BE WITNESSES IN A GLOBAL FAITH, WE HAVE TO FUNCTION LIKE MISSIONARIES.

I'll never forget the first time I heard the good news. I was sixteen, and it blew me away. Six months later, I was on the third hole of Hancock Golf Course when I finally said "yes" to Christ. By my seventeenth birthday, I was preaching somewhere almost every week—missions, street corners, and even in a few churches. Those were such wonderful times of discovery for me.

Fill in your own story here.

How about you? When did Christ first come into your life? Can you remember that awesome moment when you realized God loves you in spite of yourself? Is that moment as real to you now as it was back then?

Let me ask you another question: *When was the first time your relationship with God forced you to deal with the reality that God loves everyone just as much as he loves you—no matter what color or faith—that Christianity is not so much about you as it is about us?* You see, the good news is not just for us. The good news is not just for our church; the good news is for everyone in the world—even the Muslims, Hindus, and practioners of other faiths!

And as such, the mission of our church is about those who haven't yet heard and how we relate to them. Being members of this church doesn't entitle us to anything. In fact, it is just the opposite. We are blessed in order to bless others. We are not chosen because we are special, but we are special because we are chosen.

Do we really believe that? Or do our actions as a church suggest something else?

> A t this point, I wanted them to focus on the need for this church to have as its primary mission reaching everyone in this community for Christ and realize that each person is a missionary of Jesus Christ. I seriously wanted them to comprehend what it means to be a missionary in the U.S.

## Christianity Becomes a World Religion
### Acts 10:44-48

*While Peter was still speaking, the Holy Spirit fell upon all who heard the word. The . . . believers who had come with Peter were astounded that the gift of the Holy Spirit had been poured out even on the Gentiles. . . . Then Peter said, "Can anyone withhold the water for baptizing these people who have received the Holy Spirit just as we have?" So he ordered them to be baptized in the name of Jesus Christ.*

This event comes at the end of Peter's experience with Cornelius. Peter preaches a powerful message, and as a result, numerous people become believers and are filled with the Holy Spirit. And everyone was astonished.

Now, it's decision time. It's one thing when one or two Gentiles become followers of Jesus, as in the case of the Ethiopian—maybe those were flukes. But something is afoot when dozens of Gentiles are filled with the Holy Spirit. The door to the mission to the Gentiles has burst wide open. Now it is possible for you and me to be included in God's mission. The movement of God is fully underway. Acts 1:8 is becoming a reality.

Remember, the word *Gentile* meant anyone who wasn't Jewish. That means the door was flung open for you and me. Give that some thought. To this point in our story, the good news was mainly for the Jewish people. But no more. Christianity is becoming a world religion, and as such, it requires a different way of evangelism.

Everyone is welcome in this church. The only people who aren't welcome are those who refuse to welcome everyone else.

However, when the believers at Jerusalem heard the news, they were angry (Acts 11:1-2). How could God allow Gentiles into the faith? It's hard to believe that Christians would stand in the way of anyone receiving Christ. But they did.

> Everyone is welcome in this church. The only people who aren't welcome are those who refuse to welcome everyone else.

But here's the good part. When Peter told them how the Gentiles responded to the movement of the Holy Spirit, the criticizers rejoiced and praised God. How could they make such an about-face? Only because of their belief in God.

We may find the same true in our church as we reach out to people who are as different from us as a Gentile was from a Jew. There may be some in our midst who don't want strange people to join us. But that's their problem. They need to get over it. We can't allow anyone to get in the way of God's mission. We must realize that the good news is not about us, but about how we relate to those who have not yet responded to the good news. If they are Christians, they will do what the believers in Jerusalem did and rejoice.

So we must be clear from the start: everyone is welcome in this church. The only people who aren't welcome are those who refuse to welcome everyone else.

I didn't go into the circumcision issue, but you may want to in order to show the difference. If you do, you should compare circumcision then to nose-piercing today.

But listen to what happens next.

Around the same time as Peter was with Cornelius, converts of Philip were scattered into various parts of the world. Some of them went to Antioch and began sharing the faith with the Greeks, and many of them believed. Not long after that, the church at Antioch was born and would become a major player in the movement of God throughout the rest of the known world.

Antioch, with some 500,000 people, was the third-largest city in the Roman Empire. It was at Antioch that God's people were first called *Christians*, which means the movement was taking on an identity of its own and was no longer considered a subset of Judaism. Antioch became the launching pad for the mission to the "ends of the earth." What began at Antioch was truly the beginning of a world faith.

Starting in a major city would turn out to be Paul's strategy for all three of his missionary journeys. We live in one of the most vibrant cities in the U.S. Therefore, what we do here has the potential to ripple out to all of the country. Our mission to change the city must not fail, because its repercussion could radiate throughout the state and the nation and maybe to the "ends of the earth."

You may want to show on the screen a map of the movement of the early church. If you do, start by showing the movement from Jerusalem to the various places we've mentioned, then later in the series, show the travels of Paul. You might even want to do a flash video of the progression.

There was no going back now. The good news was unleashed into the world, just as it is going to be unleashed into our city and around the world today because we choose to be obedient and devoted to Jesus Christ.

## BACKYARD MISSIONARIES

Of course, this mission to the Gentiles is not really new. The breakthrough already occurred with Philip's witness to the Ethiopian, the conversion of Cornelius, and the evangelization of the city of Antioch. What is new is that, for the first time, a local church saw the need for a witness beyond it, to the larger world, and commissioned missionaries to carry out that task. The church at Antioch became the first "sending church" in Christianity. And that is what I'm asking you to do—to commission backyard missionaries to our city, because if we are going to transform our city, we are going to have to think and act like missionaries.

But I can hear you say, "I can't be a missionary and quit my job and go to a foreign country." I agree—you can't do that. And I'm not asking you to do that. So rest easy.

Suppose I told you that being a missionary doesn't require you to quit your job or go to a foreign country. Suppose I could convince you that you can be a missionary in your own backyard? Would that change your mind? Would that open up a world of new possibilities for serving Christ and becoming a blessing to others?

The U.S. is less Christian today than at any other time in its history.

When most people hear the word *missionary* they think of someone going off to a foreign country. That used to be the case—but no more. Today, we are called to be "backyard missionaries" to our networks. Let me show you why.

> Your people may have a problem understanding how the term *missionary* applies to them, so you will need to set the stage for their understanding. You may want to use all or some of the following.

Today, only 30 percent of all missionaries are being sent away from the U.S. In fact, Africa, Latin America, and Korea send out the most missionaries—most of them to the U.S. because North America is now one of the least Christian areas in the world. Every day, the gap between Christian and non-Christian grows.

> # The U.S. is less Christian today than at any other time in its history.

During the final five years of the 1990s, Christianity grew between 7 and 8 percent worldwide, compared to only 1 percent between 1965 and 1985. Currently 165,000 people every day around the world are, for the first time, claiming Christ. At the current rate, within just a few years one half of the world will be Christian. That's almost four billion people! Yet in North America, Christianity continues to decline in actual numbers and percentage of the population.

In 1948, when Gallup began tracking religious identification, the percentage who claimed to be Christian was 91 percent.[1] Today, less than 75 percent of Americans claim to be Christians. Fifteen percent claim no religious affiliation at all, and the number is growing every year. In 1972, Gallup measured 5 percent with "no religion." According to CNN, "America is a less Christian nation than it was 20 years ago, and Christianity is not losing out to other religions, but primarily to a rejection of religion altogether."[2]

According to a Fox News report, in 2009 the number of people who claim no religious affiliation, meanwhile, had doubled since 1990 to 15 percent, its highest point in history. Nonbelievers now represent the third-largest group of Americans, after Catholics and Baptists. The American Religious Identification Survey (ARIS) reveals that Protestants now represent half of all Americans, down almost 20 percent in the last twenty years. In the coming months, America will become a minority Protestant nation for the first time since the pilgrims.

Nearly a quarter of Americans in their 20s profess no organized religion.

If these trends continue, by the midpoint of the twenty-first century it will be difficult to call the U.S. a Christian nation. Already in the eyes of the world, the U.S. is one of the largest mission fields. More missionaries are now sent to the U.S. than from the U.S. The last time I looked, the U.S. was the third-highest nation receiving missionaries from other countries. Thus, those Christians who share their faith will be more like missionaries than they would like to think.

So this is one of the most critical points in the story both of the U.S. and of Acts. If we are going to transform our city, we have to do like Paul and become missionaries, but not on foreign soil. We must become missionaries in our own backyard.

You may find that some church people don't think these statistics apply to their area, especially if they live in a rural area. They will insist that most people in the area are churched in some way. But I assure you, there isn't anywhere in the Western Hemisphere where the majority of people are in church. So you may have to look into the stats for your specific area. Two good companies to give you this information are Percept[3] and MissionInsite.[4]

If you need more help here, you might want to use the two metaphors I used in my book *Ministry in Hard Times*. In the book, I contrast two metaphors—the National Park World and the Jungle World. The National Park world is characterized by Ozzie and Harriet, and the Jungle World is characterized by Ozzy Osbourne. Your people have to realize that they no longer live in the 1950s. Between 1954, with the advent of Bill Haley's "Rock Around the Clock," and September 11, 2001, the world has experienced a radical break with the past. Not much will be the same ever again, including the way Christians must live out their lives in the world.

Missionaries have to do three things:
- Learn a new language
- Learn a new culture
- Learn a new technology

Missionaries have to do three things to reach a strange and new culture. They have to learn a new language, a new culture, and a new technology. We know a missionary to China needs to learn Chinese. We also understand the need to avoid shaking hands if you are a missionary to Japan. We also understand that if we are in the backwoods of somewhere we don't whip out our PowerPoint. When in Rome, we must do as the Romans do, without compromising the gospel. If we are to reach our city, we must first understand how the nonbeliever in our city thinks, feels, and needs.

That's why we need to spend more time with unchurched people than we do with our churched friends. I know. You don't want to do that, but we must if we are to be backyard missionaries. Studies show that once people have been churched for more than three years, the odds are, they no longer have any non-Christian friends. We can't let that happen to us if we want to change our city for Christ.

## WE MUST THINK AND ACT LIKE MISSIONARIES
### (ACTS 17:16-23)

*Then Paul stood in front of the Areopagus and said, "Athenians, I see how extremely religious you are in every way. For as I went through the city and looked carefully at the objects of your worship, I found among them an altar with the inscription, 'To an unknown god.' What therefore you worship as unknown, this I proclaim to you."* (Acts 17:22-23)

Paul gives us an example here of how missionaries think. One of his missionary journeys took him to Athens, where he preached before the Council of City Elders. They wanted to know what strange new faith he was teaching. But before he preached, he surveyed the culture, looking for ways to couch his message in the language and culture of the Athenians. He hit upon the statue to the unknown God and he then proclaimed that God to be the God of Jesus Christ, who is above all other gods.

The culture of that day was extremely polytheistic, much like our culture today. They believed in many gods, just like we do today. Although their gods were made of stone, our gods are more subtle—money, fame, power, glory, revenge.

On his way to the Areopagus, which was the high court of appeals for criminal and civil cases, Paul had to pass by hundreds of stone gods. No other place on earth at the time had so many idols on exhibition. But Paul went right for the jugular vein and proclaimed the God of Jesus Christ to be above all other gods.

The same is true in the U.S. To reach the new, emerging world, we have to think and act differently. We have to learn a new language (Rock 'n' Roll); we have to learn a new culture (causal and post-Christian); and we have to learn a new technology (digital). We have to become backyard missionaries.

This is also why we must change the way we worship. We can't continue to use music that hurts the ears of today's culture. We can't continue using words that only seasoned Christians understand. We have to speak the gospel in the language that skeptical, unchurched people understand if we want to communicate successfully with them. We have to incorporate the music and the language of the twenty-first century if we want to be backyard missionaries.

Whether you go ahead and say, "and that means Rock 'n' Roll music," is up to your situation. But keep in mind that there is no use waving a red flag in front of a bull until you're ready for a fight.

Like first-century Christianity, Christianity today is in a more hostile environment than ever before, and therefore, Christians have to think and act like missionaries.

## BEING MISSIONARIES ISN'T EASY
### (ACTS 1–6; 15:5-12)

I've combined an early portion of Acts with a middle portion of it to show a continuing flaw in the disciples. You could easily make one, stand-alone message out of this section, especially if you anticipate a lot of push-back from the congregation about being missionaries.

We're not the only ones having trouble being backyard missionaries. The early church in Jerusalem did too. And it teetered on the brink of making the same three fatal mistakes many churches make today.

If we revisit the first six chapters of Acts, we find the early disciples hunkered down in Jerusalem, about to make a fatal mistake. Instead of figuring out how to take the good news to the rest of the world, as Jesus commanded them to do, they focused their attention on organizing the Jerusalem church. Instead of preparing missionaries to leave the church and go out into the world with the message of Christ, they began to organize and structure the church to be able to take care of itself. Choosing Stephen to care for the widows and orphans is one example (Acts 6).

Y ou may want to unpack this story in a way that shows how the church was hunkering down and focusing on itself but the Holy Spirit wouldn't let it.

After Pentecost, for several years the disciples hunkered down in Jerusalem and built a congregation. Of course there is nothing wrong with taking care of the church, but not at the expense of spreading the good news. The problem was that this new congregation didn't have a strategy for taking Christianity global. It was not taking Jesus' last will and testament seriously. The early church acted much like declining churches today—they focused on the care and feeding of themselves and the consequences were nearly fatal, since that is not what God intended for his people. Our own church can no longer afford to make this fatal mistake.

Sure, widows and orphans need caring for, but the care and feeding of the church can never be the only priority of a church. Not when Jesus commanded us to "go therefore and make disciples of all nations" (Matt. 28:19).

Actually, there are two commands of Jesus we must follow above all else—the Great Commandment and the Great Commission. One has to do with taking care of others, and the other has to do with sharing the good news. So we need to keep this in mind—we can care for people without transforming them, but we can't transform people without first caring for them. It's important to feed the body, but it's more important to feed the body *and* the soul. We must do both. We can't focus on one without the other.

The second mistake made by the early church is the way it responded to the complainers. Some of the church members complained that they were not being treated fairly. They were not getting their full membership benefits. A feeling of entitlement was building up within the congregation. People began to feel entitled to God's grace, rather than being the agents of God's grace. So instead of sending out their newly trained leadership to start new churches and become missionaries in the world, they appointed some of their best leaders to meet the needs of the complainers.

God sought to correct the problem by making Philip a missionary and making Stephen a martyr. And then came the last straw—Herod began persecuting the Christians, and as a result, the early church members were dispersed throughout the region and became reluctant missionaries after all.

But even with the persecution, the apostles did not leave Jerusalem. It took a vision from God to Peter and a missionary to the Gentiles named Paul to finally convince them that they were called to be missionaries, not caretakers.

Sound familiar? Have we also made those mistakes in the past? Those two bad strategic decisions have been duplicated by the church for centuries. Down through the years, churches have failed to reach beyond themselves into a new world, and they have became ingrown. They've used their human resources to comfort the complainers who emerged in the ingrown church. We cannot afford to continue this mistake. It's time for the complainers to shape up or ship out. This isn't our church—we don't own it, and we're not entitled to its benefits. It's God's church, and we are its stewards.

## ACTS 15:5-12

*But some believers who belonged to the sect of the Pharisees stood up and said, "It is necessary for them to be circumcised and ordered to keep the law of Moses."*

*The apostles and the elders met together to consider this matter. After there had been much debate, Peter stood up and said to them, "My brothers, you know that in the early days God made a choice among you, that I should be the one through whom the Gentiles would hear the message of the good news and become believers. And God, who knows the human heart, testified to them by giving them the Holy Spirit, just as he did to us; and in cleansing their hearts by faith he has made no distinction between them and us. Now therefore why are you putting God to the test by placing on the neck of the disciples a yoke that neither our ancestors nor we have been able to bear? On the contrary, we believe that we will be saved through the grace of the Lord Jesus, just as they will."*

*The whole assembly kept silence, and listened to Barnabas and Paul as they told of all the signs and wonders that God had done through them among the Gentiles.*

The third almost fatal mistake of the early church occured here at the Jerusalem Conference, one of the most pivotal times in the life of the early church. The Apostle Paul encountered thousands of converts in his ministry in the church at Antioch. However, in doing so, he violated one of the cherished traditions of Judaism—he did not make them become Jews first, through the rite of circumcision. The leaders at Jerusalem were hanging on to the old baggage of Judaism. It would be much like us saying that if you're not a baptized member of our church, you aren't a Christian. That totally negates the grace of God. You and I are saved by grace and nothing more. Salvation is a gift that we can't ever earn or deserve. Certainly it's not something we can attain through some dumb ritual.

So the elders at Jerusalem sent a man named Barnabas down to sniff out what was going on in Antioch. And guess what? Barnabas was so captured by the movement of God that he not only began to minister to the Gentiles but also enlisted the services of Paul, and the Church in Antioch exploded.

In time, Barnabas reported to the Jerusalem church that Gentiles were converting to Christianity in record numbers. So the elders at Jerusalem had a powwow, much like the church conference we're going to have in the near future, where we will decide if we are really ready to bite the bullet and pull out all of the stops to make this a great church with thousands of people. This powwow was called the Jerusalem Conference. It was there that Peter showed his true colors and finally said salvation is by grace alone. After Paul and Barnabas told their story, the elders sat silent. Their decision was for the Gentiles to abstain from certain items used in pagan worship.

Why did Peter take this stand? Because God had prepared him for it when God forced him to go to Cornelius. There Peter saw, for the first time, God working a miracle in the life of a non-Jew. Peter was so sold-out to the mission of God that he wouldn't let anything stand in the way of another person experiencing this wonder, no matter that person's race or culture.

Even the hunkered-down Jerusalem church melted when it heard how many Gentiles were coming to Christ as a result of Paul breaking one of its most sacred rules. And I expect the same kind of Christian response from our board when people complain about the changes we're making. Nothing is more important than people giving their lives to Christ.

My friends, if a Jew can drop his most sacred ritual for the cause of Christ, you and I ought to be able to change worship styles to reach out to people we don't know. It's time for us to quit bickering about the changes we've made in worship and act like mature Christians who will do anything to advance the cause of Christ. For, you see, the gospel is not about you and me. It's about what we do with it on behalf of others.

Now, if you think the changes we've made are radical, wait until you see the next service we're going to start when this service fills up.

Friends, let's be honest. The issue at the Jerusalem Conference wasn't the Jewish rite, but rather, "Can we really believe that our lifelong enemies are also the object of God's love?" Or, "Can we really worship with people who are totally different from us?" But that's the whole point of the good news—that all people, even those we don't like, are equal recipients of God's love. The role of any Christian is to invite them to feast on that love. Aren't you glad that's true—because you and I wouldn't be here today otherwise?

We stand today in the same place as Peter. God is asking us to relieve ourselves of some of our baggage—our rituals, our prejudices, our personal preferences in worship, our _____ (you fill in the blank). What will our response be? Will we allow the mission of Christ to be so real in our lives that we have to say with Peter, "God makes no distinction between us and them"? Or, "I'll be happy with any form of worship, program, policy, or structure if it brings more people to Christ"? How could our response be anything else if we love Jesus? It can't! It just simply can't. Not if we love Jesus more than ourselves.

We must never allow rules and regulations to get in our way of spreading the good news. We must never allow traditions, no matter how sacred to us, to stand in the way of bringing people to Christ. One of those traditions that we must wean ourselves from is our commitment to using the hymns in the hymnal, even if no one knows the hymns anymore. It's time we did away with the hymnal and, in its place, substitute songs that people know, even if they are secular songs that have spiritual meaning.

Isn't that the real issue? Who do we love the most—ourselves or God?

I f you are in a situation where a multicultural church is called for, this section of Acts is crucial for you, so you may want to expand on it. The church at Antioch comprised all kinds of people from many races. God's blessing on inclusive evangelism across ethnic lines at Antioch is a necessary reminder of where God's heart is. While God may indeed give growth within homogeneous ethnic units, such growth is not the only way the gospel can spread. In fact, in a multicultural environment it is not the best way for the gospel to spread.

From Antioch, Paul and others spread the good news across the region. Thousands of Gentiles heard and responded. It was not long before Paul began his three missionary journeys, and the movement of God spread over the land.

The same thing happens today when people give themselves to the mission of Christ and reach out to those in need of good news. More people are won to Christ when we leave the church than when we hide behind its four walls. It's time we developed a serious plan for reaching our city with the good news.

But listen to what happens to churches that hunker down and care only for themselves. The Jerusalem church fell on hard times. Later in Paul's writings, we learn that he has had to take up a collection from all of his church plants to keep the church at Jerusalem from going under. Churches that hunker down and take care of themselves grow weak. If we continue to focus solely on ourselves, we too will wind up broke—spiritually and financially.

You may want to compare the reactions of Peter and Paul to the mission of the church. At first, Peter hunkered down in the Jerusalem church, whereas Paul was always on the road to mission with Jesus. A major part of this story is the struggle Peter experienced before he went to see Cornelius. Remember, Peter was a key leader in the Jerusalem church, and clearly the leading apostle based on Jesus' own feelings toward him. Peter was responsible for the Jerusalem church's hunkering down and focusing on internal things—like organizing the church—when he should have been on the road to mission with Jesus. Paul, on the other hand, was always on the road to mission with Jesus. Peter might also be compared to someone who grew up in the church and was therefore always aware of God's love, since Peter had spent so much time with Jesus. Paul, on the other hand, grew up a slave to legalism rather than grace and, as such, had a much more burning passion for those who had not yet experienced such grace. This might also explain why new converts to the faith are usually more on fire for evangelism than long-term Christians.

## TIME TO TALK TURKEY

We have a problem in our church. Some of our present leaders are acting much like those in Jerusalem. They don't seem to care if the church grows, at least not by conversion growth. They want it to remain a close-knit social club of do-gooders, where everyone looks alike, smells alike, and acts alike. I want everyone to hear this—that kind of attitude isn't welcome anymore. It simply isn't welcome here anymore. The church exists not for us, but for those who aren't yet part of our church. It's not about you and me. It's about them and about how much God loves them.

So listen carefully—everyone is welcome here who welcomes everyone else. If you don't welcome everyone else, you aren't welcome here anymore, from this day forward (this phrase stuck with the good people and became the seed-bed for our value of inclusion). You will have to take your bigotry somewhere else.

Needless to say, some were not happy at this point in the message. Keep in mind that, at this point in the turnaround, we still didn't have many visitors in worship. I would not preach this way if the church had lots of visitors. I would do it in board meetings.

## TAKING IT HOME

> ## Will you join us this Saturday in going door to door?

So, I put the question before you—will we open our doors to people we don't know, understand, or even like? Will we have the same missionary spirit as those who were scattered abroad after the stoning of Stephen? Or will we continue to hunker down in the bunker of this nice, cozy social club? The choice is ours, but as for me, I'm going to go out each day and night of every week to be with the modern-day Gentile until this room is so full, it's uncomfortable.

Beginning next Saturday, the small group I've been meeting with on Friday nights is going to begin going door to door every Saturday asking people one question—"What it is that you need from the churches in your area that you aren't getting?" I'm inviting you to join us this coming Saturday to walk the neighborhood for Christ and, in the example of Philip, Peter, Paul, and Barnabas, continue to spread the good news to everyone in our area. Will you join us this Saturday as we fling open the door for everyone in San Antonio?

Does this give you any ideas?

# NOTES

1. http://www.gallup.com/poll/117409/easter-smaller-percentage-americans-christian.aspx.

2. http://www.cnn.com/2009/LIVING/wayoflife/03/09/us.religion.less.christian/.

3. http://www.perceptgroup.com/.

4. http://www.missioninsite.com/.

CHAPTER 8

# IT'S NOT ABOUT YOU OR ME; IT'S ABOUT THE KINGDOM

## KEY IDEA

GOD WANTS STRONG CHURCHES THAT CAN CHANGE SOCIETY.

You could easily turn this chapter into two messages—one on what it means to be a strong church and another on what it means to be an Acts 1:8 church. Or you may want to combine the two ideas.

By now, I am about eight months into the restart of the church. I have trained a small cadre of leaders, and we have canvassed about 2,000 homes to listen to the residents' concerns.[1] A board meeting is scheduled to vote on a proposal that will change the course of the church and begin it on its slow climb to become one of the largest churches in south Texas. One part of the proposal is to borrow enough money to begin a pre-school, and another is to radically change the style of worship. What I will learn that night is that half of the present attendees will leave as a result of this evening. It's show time.

Our reading about the life of the early church should have taught us one thing by now about how strong churches function. If we want to be the authentic church of Jesus Christ, we must be willing to give ourselves on behalf of our God, our neighbors, and one another. Every example from Acts so far has shown us that authentic Christianity is lived outwardly on behalf of others, not selfishly—that to be authentic, the church has to be focused more outwardly than inwardly. This means that everything we do as a people should be to honor God, to reach out in love to our neighbor, and to support one another. No church can achieve favor with God by caring for itself more than it cares for those who are not yet with us.

> # The primary thrust of our church must be outward to the neighborhood, community, and world.

Therefore, the primary thrust of our church must be outward, not inward. We must evaluate every issue by how it will honor God, transform our neighbor, and unite us in love. We must never make the mistake most of the congregations are making today—we must never make the survival of our church the main goal. God doesn't care if our church survives, but God passionately cares if our church is on his mission to transform the world.

We know one other key truth from Acts—God's church can change the course of history. And I believe God will do that through our church if we ask him.

I know—we're still facing bankruptcy, and many of you are afraid to take any more risks. But mark it well—God honors those who honor God. What you have been doing the past few years has not honored God; you have been focused on survival. You should know by now that with God's help we are changing that direction. From now on, we must cease worrying about survival and go on the offensive for the Kingdom. It is time we became a church and closed the social club.

### Acts 15:36–18:31

With the Jerusalem Conference out of the way, Paul soon began his three missionary journeys to plant churches in the major cities. It was not his nature to linger long in any one place. His goal was to make strong churches that would change the world.

The same is true today. God's mission is to make strong churches that make the world a different place. That is the essence of the rest of Acts. As such, strong churches:

- challenge the evils of society
- use the culture in order to reach the culture
- grow and make no excuse for their growth
- know that being on the road to mission with Jesus is the primary ministry of the church
- prepare themselves to suffer for the gospel

Now, let's take a look at each of these five points.

"He went through Syria and Cilicia, strengthening the churches" (Acts 15:41).

"So the churches were strengthened in the faith and increased in numbers daily" (Acts 16:5).

The rest of Acts consists of Paul's missionary journeys and the expansion of the Kingdom. Paul revisits all of the churches he had been in previously with one purpose in mind—to make them stronger.

H ere, the map discussed earlier would be a great visual image of the spread of the early church, or you could find several of them at: http://www.ccel.org/bible/phillips/CN092MAPS1.htm.

That's God's desire for our church—that we be strong enough to do what the early churches did—change the course of society. We're not just building a church; we're building a people who will change one another and the city. We're not concerned about members; we're concerned about making disciples who will turn this city upside down. We're not concerned about our survival anymore. Now, we are concerned about being an instrument of God for the good of those around us.

We shouldn't be concerned about the naysayers; we should be listening to the voice of God. We shouldn't worry about the cost, because Jesus didn't worry about the cost of our redemption.

I'm asking you to join me tonight in casting your vote for the advancement of the Kingdom, not the survival of the church. God wants this church to be strong and vibrant. God wants this church to change the city. And I'm asking you to join me in that quest.

Now, I want you to notice a few things about strong churches that make the world a different place.

STRONG CHURCHES CHALLENGE THE EVILS OF SOCIETY
(ACTS 16:16-40)

*One day, as we were going to the place of prayer, we met a slave girl who had a spirit of divination and brought her owners a great deal of money by fortune-telling. While she followed Paul and us, she would cry out, "These men are slaves of the Most High God, who proclaim to you a way of salvation." She kept doing this for many days. But Paul, very much annoyed, turned and said to the spirit, "I order you in the name of Jesus Christ to come out of her." And it came out that very hour.*

*But when her owners saw that their hope of making money was gone, they seized Paul and Silas and dragged them into the marketplace before the authorities. When they had brought them before the magistrates, they said, "These men are disturbing our city; they are Jews and are advocating customs that are not lawful for us as Romans to adopt or observe." The crowd joined in attacking them, and the magistrates had them stripped of their clothing and ordered them to be beaten with rods.* (Acts 16:16-22)

You might also choose another text to show this point, then talk about any events in the life of your church in the past where this might have happened.

You should notice two things in this text. One, Paul focused on the spiritual plight of the people before he addressed the physical injustices. In fact, some would say he dragged his feet before he addressed the social issues. Two, even though it put him at great risk, when the time was right, he healed the demented girl and upset the financial apple cart of that city.

For some in the congregation, the key here is, "when the time is right." For those of you who are concerned about the social ills of society, I promise you the day will come when this church will exercise an immense influence on the actions of this city. But for now, we will put this part of our ministry on hold until we are strong enough to make a difference. Anything we might attempt at this point in time would simply make our future less bright as a church.

There were a number of people who felt strongly about social justice. That was all the church had done the last five years. Unfortunately the people who were focused on social justice alone were the first to leave when we began focusing on Jesus. A shame, since social justice became one of our strongest ministries the last half of my twenty-four-year ministry among them.

You should keep in mind that unless you are an African-American or Hispanic church, or an inner-city church, you should avoid social issues until you are strong enough to withstand the conflict. We waited some ten years before we entered the social justice arena, but when we did, we were strong enough to make a huge difference.

## STRONG CHURCHES USE THE CULTURE IN ORDER TO REACH THE CULTURE
### (ACTS 17:22-31)

I took some time here because it was the foundation for changing the worship style.

*Then Paul stood in front of the Areopagus and said, "Athenians, I see how extremely religious you are in every way. For as I went through the city and looked carefully at the objects of your worship, I found among them an altar with the inscription, 'To an unknown god.' What therefore you worship as unknown, this I proclaim to you."* (Acts 17:22-23)

Paul understood something very important. He understood the importance of knowing the culture in which you are sharing the good news. He had walked through the city and could not help noticing the hundreds of idols to their gods. But the one cultural clue that gave him an opening into their world was the idol to the unknown god. He used that idol as a way into sharing the good news.

We must not be afraid of using parts of the culture to reach culture. Nowhere is this truer than in the way we worship. Our worship must reflect the culture, so that people are comfortable enough to hear the dangerous gospel. I promise you—I will not water down or change the gospel. It will remain the same, but our worship style and the way we offer hospitality must change, so that the unchurched feel comfortable enough to hear the dangerous gospel.

If the vote passes tonight, next Sunday's worship will be different. And I remind you, no form of worship is presented in the Scriptures as the most authentic. Just think of the style of worship as the package in which the gospel is presented. Don't confuse the style with the essence. Worship must be done in a way that people can experience God through it. That can't happen if worship feels foreign to them.

For some churches, you and your people may need to spend more time out in the culture to really know it. Don't just assume you know it. This is especially true in rural areas that are being encroached upon by the big city.

STRONG CHURCHES GROW AND MAKE NO EXCUSE FOR THEIR GROWTH

Everywhere Paul went on his journeys, he experienced conversions and found already established Christians. As a result, he left strong churches behind.

I'm tired of those people who say they want the church to remain small. I'm tired of those people who say they don't think we should be concerned with numbers. I'm tired of those people who say all I'm about is building my own little kingdom. I'm tired of my colleagues who say I water down the gospel in order to grow. The Bible is clear: strong churches add to their numbers daily. If you don't believe that and aren't willing to pray for that to happen, then you should find another church. It's just that simple, because this church is going to be faithful and grow!

And we're not going to do this simply to become big. We're going to accomplish it because that is the mandate Jesus placed on all of us—to make disciples. If we make disciples, this church and other churches around us will grow. It's just that simple. People who want their church to remain small simply don't understand the mandate Jesus placed on us. And it's time they get with Jesus' program.

STRONG CHURCHES KNOW THAT BEING ON THE ROAD TO MISSION WITH
JESUS IS THE PRIMARY MINISTRY OF THE CHURCH

I made reference to the fact that most of the rest of Acts is about Paul's missionary journeys.

If we are to be faithful to the gospel, most of our ministry will have an outward thrust to it. We must gauge our success by how many adult baptisms we have, by how many recommitments of faith we see, by how many missionaries we produce, and by how many members see their primary ministry as being in their workplace or playground or family. This means our mission is not how many members we have or how big we become. It means our mission is about growing a people who will transform a city. That's our goal. And I think it's one worth sacrificing for. It's one I'm willing to risk my ministry among you on.

## STRONG CHURCHES ARE PREPARED TO SUFFER FOR THE GOSPEL
### (ACTS 16:25-40)

*About midnight Paul and Silas were praying and singing hymns to God, and the prisoners were listening to them. Suddenly there was an earthquake, so violent that the foundations of the prison were shaken; and immediately all the doors were opened and everyone's chains were unfastened. When the jailer woke up and saw the prison doors wide open, he drew his sword and was about to kill himself, since he supposed that the prisoners had escaped. But Paul shouted in a loud voice, "Do not harm yourself, for we are all here." The jailer called for lights, and rushing in, he fell down trembling before Paul and Silas. Then he brought them outside and said, "Sirs, what must I do to be saved?" They answered, "Believe on the Lord Jesus, and you will be saved, you and your household." They spoke the word of the Lord to him and to all who were in his house. At the same hour of the night he took them and washed their wounds; then he and his entire family were baptized without delay. He brought them up into the house and set food before them; and he and his entire household rejoiced that he had become a believer in God. (Acts 16:25-34)*

Several times during the last few years of Paul's life, he was persecuted and even thrown into jail. The one experience that always captivates me is when Paul and Silas are thrown into jail in Philippi. While awaiting their sentence, three things happened: they sang praises to God; the doors of the jail burst open; and the jailer asked, "What must I do to be saved?" You see—suffering isn't always what it appears to be. Sometimes, it's the prelude to salvation. The interesting thing about the text is that Paul isn't surprised by the jailer's response. And neither should we be when someone responds favorably to our witness. It's part of God's plan.

My friends, what we will propose tonight is worth suffering for. And believe me, if you adopt the proposal, it will cause all of us some suffering. For some, the suffering may be the loss of some friendships; for others, it will be the loss of some church heritages that are dear to you; but for all who choose to go forward with this proposal, the suffering will be financial. We will all have to decide how much the mission is worth.

It's time to show what we're made of. It's time to quit hunkering down and begin reaching out to all of San Antonio. It's time to be a church once again.

## PREPARE FOR OPPOSITION
### (ACTS 20:28-32)

*Keep watch over yourselves and over all the flock, of which the Holy Spirit has made you overseers, to shepherd the church of God that he obtained with the blood of his own Son. I know that after I have gone, savage wolves will come in among you, not sparing the flock. Some even from your own group will come distorting the truth in order to entice the disciples to follow them. Therefore be alert, remembering that for three years I did not cease night or day to warn everyone with tears. And now I commend you to God and to the message of his grace, a message that is able to build you up and to give you the inheritance among all who are sanctified.*

All through the travels of Paul, the Jews kept attacking him and the churches he'd planted because they were threatening the Jews' way of life. The same is true today. During our journey toward transformation, we've found that some church members, both in our church and in other churches, oppose what we are attempting to accomplish. And we have done what Paul did—we have ignored them in love. We must respond to them in love, because they are ignorant of what God is doing in our midst. And if opposition arises again tonight, keep your cool and focus your attention on all of the new people God will bring our way.

I pray tonight will go well. I pray all of us will handle ourselves as children of God. I look forward to seeing you tonight.

Now, keep in mind that we had done our homework. We knew all of the highly respected leaders of the church were behind the proposal we would bring to the board that night. If they all showed up and stood their ground, it would all be over. So do your homework, because I guarantee you, the opposition will do its homework. Hopefully, you won't have any opposition.

Also, keep in mind that if your church is having a lot of visitors, you may want to preach only the positive parts of this series and save the negative parts for your board meetings. That way, you don't run off the visitors.

## TAKING IT HOME
### (ACTS 28:30-31)

Luke ends Acts where he began—with the Ever-widening Circle. Listen to the last words of Acts: "[Paul] lived there two whole years at his own expense and welcomed all who came to him, proclaiming the kingdom of God and teaching about the Lord Jesus Christ with all boldness and without hindrance" (Acts 28:30-31).

Paul is now in Rome, under house arrest, but he is still able to share the good news without any constraints.

Like Paul, our door must always be open to the stranger, our welcome mat must always be out, and our message must always be about Jesus Christ. We have no other option; we have no other message; and we urgently must share it with our neighbors.

Luke abruptly ends Acts with Paul imprisoned in his home in Rome, with no hint of what happens to Paul. I would love to know the rest of the story, wouldn't you? But Luke has done what he set out to do—to show the movement of Christianity to the four corners of the known world—to show how a faith that began in a tiny corner of Palestine had, in less than thirty years, spread all the way to Rome. Now, the rest is up to us. Luke didn't finish the story because he couldn't. We have to put our own finishing touches to the story. And Christians around the world, from now on, will do their part in finishing the story.

That's awesome. You and I can have a part in putting the finishing touches to the most life-changing movement in history. All we have to do is be a witness to Jesus Christ, with those like us and those unlike us, in our backyard, our nation, and our world.

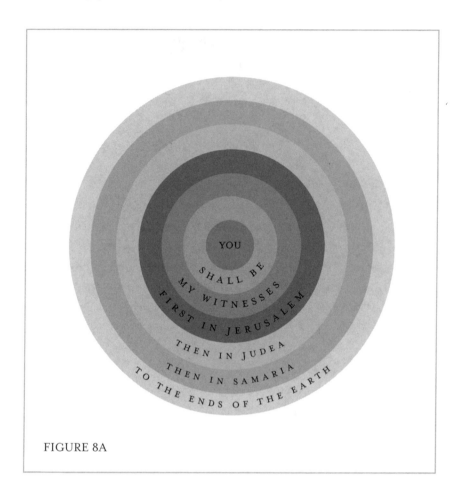

FIGURE 8A

So we end our series where we began months ago—with Acts 1:8 and the Ever-widening Circle. Take a look at it one more time (put the graphic on the screen). See the outward flow?

Now, put the graphic up with the arrow pointing from the church to the world.

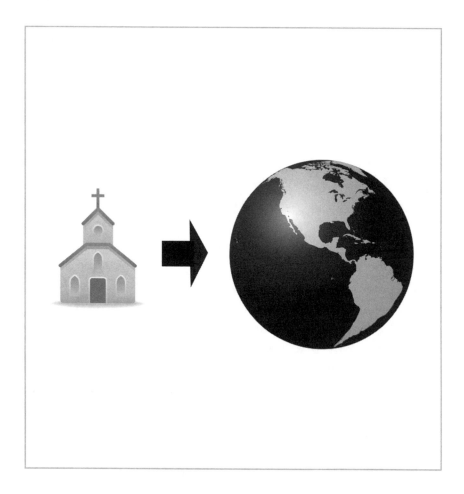

Now, take a look at this picture. This is what God expects of us. Not for us to attract people to our building, but for us to go out to them and share the good news right where they are.

God is calling us to be his witnesses—to give our lives on behalf of our church, our city, our nation, those whom we don't even like, and the entire world. We can do no less and be God's church.

## ACTS 1:8 CHURCH

We have seen what it means to be an Acts 1:8 church. So that all of us are clear and there are no misconceptions about what it means to be an Acts 1:8 church, let me nail down the meaning in the most practical terms.

After each of the following, be prepared to offer a practical, concrete step for your people to make that part of Acts 1:8 come true in your church or neighborhood.

Being an Acts 1:8 church means we must commission more people to be ambassadors for Christ in their neighborhoods and playgrounds than we nominate to fill offices or ministries within our church. Ours is not an inward-grown faith. Take a look at the Acts 1:8 graphic. God is always pointing us outward, toward the world, and never inward, toward ourselves. The place to begin is by reducing the number of people nominated to serve on committees in the church and by making sure that we commission more people to the community than to the church. I know this transition will take some time, but we must begin now. So beginning in January, I propose we eliminate the worship or evangelism committee and nominate five people to begin five small groups in their homes.

Being an Acts 1:8 church means we must develop more ministries out where people live and work than we develop programs at church where we expect people to attend. The primary ministry of the early church wasn't done in a building or centered around institutional needs. It was done where the people live. We must not sit and wait for the world to come to us; we must go to the world, because we are by nature a sent church. So within the next month, I'm inviting all of you to join me each Saturday in canvassing the neighborhood (remember this was in 1969).

Being an Acts 1:8 church means we must place more emphasis on those who have not yet heard the good news than on those of us who pay the bills. Entitlement to a church, a pastor, or membership privileges is not God's way; it is the devil's way. We must take up the meaning of the word *witness,* and become modern-day martyrs for Christ. So beginning in three months, I will begin inviting some of you to join me in my home visits to newcomers.

Being an Acts 1:8 church means we are more concerned with the community, the unwanted, and the world than we are with our buildings and programs. Yes, we will have building programs in our future, but they will never occupy the bulk of our time, energy, and money. So next year, depending on the vote tonight, we will begin a Christian preschool, designed to reach into the community. We will also adopt the Colonial Hills Elementary School and offer tutoring after hours.

Being an Acts 1:8 church means we must spend more time in our communities and networks doing our part to be witnesses for Christ than we do at church attending meetings or going to worship. So I'm encouraging you to never spend more than a couple of hours a week on these premises so you will have time to spend with your networks.

Being an Acts 1:8 church means we must concern ourselves more with the injustices perpetrated on those who cannot defend themselves than we do on securing the benefits of church membership. We cannot allow it to continue to flood the Westside every time it rains or when too many of us flush our toilets at the same time (you can fill in here an example from your community). So I will be encouraging you to join with some other churches in "Project Free" (the forerunner to Meals on Wheels) and when we are healthy to engage in community action to help those who can't help themselves.

Being an Acts 1:8 church means we must focus more on expanding the kingdom of God rather than on building a church. Our church is just one of the many signs of the Kingdom that God has placed on this earth. We must always keep that in mind—it is God's church, not ours. So I promise whatever building we do in the future will be simple and inexpensive, leaving us money to promote the gospel.

Being an Acts 1:8 church means that God is the subject on which the church dotes, not us. God is the subject; we are the worshipers. Theology calls this the *Imago Dei,* the "image of God."[2] If we want to be on God's mission, we must ask the following questions:

- What is God up to these days?
- What is God up to in our neighborhood, our city, our nation, and the world?
- What does God want to do, and are we the ones keeping it from happening?
- What does God need from us, not what do we need from God?

Such questions keep the church from focusing on us. They help us to focus on God and his Kingdom and our part in it. It takes us out of the area of selfish church entitlement and places us squarely in the path of what God is about in our world. It removes the inward, self-centered forms of organized religion. It drives us out of the safety of these four walls and into the everyday world of the ordinary and mundane.

Such questions are the reasons a dozen or more of us have been canvassing our neighborhood, asking questions about what's up in residents' lives. Such questions are driving the upcoming board meeting and vote on our future.

**I'm not asking you to do church differently; I'm asking you to be the church for the first time.** That's a scary thought—to be the church for the first time. I know some of you have been in church most of your lives, but being in church and being the church aren't necessarily the same. Being the church in the world is what God is calling every Christian to do.

---

# The Big Shift:
## From asking how better to grow our church to asking what God is up to in our neighborhood

---

Look again at the Acts 1:8 graphic. Notice the center of the circles—it's you and me. And notice how Jesus forces us to move our thoughts away from us and into the world. That's the kind of church I'm praying we become—a church on God's mission, not a church on our mission. I'm praying we become a church focused on finding what God is up to in the world and asking him to allow us to be a part of it.

**Now, let me show you the big shift I'm asking you to make. Instead of asking, *"What we must do to attract more people to our worship?"* I'm asking us to begin asking, "What is God up to in our neighborhood, and how do we need to change to be part of it?"** Do you see the difference? It is as different as night from day. It takes the focus off of us and places it squarely on God. When we do that, our community of faith will explode with new converts.

And the irony of all of this is the more we focus on these aspects of Christianity, the stronger our church will become, and the more influence our witnessing will have in our neighborhoods and the city.

So pray this prayer with me this morning:

*God, show us what you are about in our city and what you want to see happen. Then, run over us with that mission; pound us into the ground if you have to, until we willingly and joyfully seek to be a part of your mission.*

POSTLUDE

That fateful night forty people showed up. We had had only thirty-seven in worship that morning. The vote was 21-19, in favor of a new direction. Over the next few months, most of the nineteen left the church. I felt bad about that then; today, I don't. Now I know those people were the primary problem. (They probably are in your church also.)

Please be sure that whatever you do, you do it in love. Don't copy what I did. I had nothing to lose. Do what you are comfortable doing. But remember, there is more to life than changing spiritual diapers.

If nothing else, if you catch the passion of the type of messages that will move a church off dead-center, this book has served its purpose. Now, go out and get the job of transformation done.

# NOTES

1. While canvassing, we asked each person we visited what he or she needed most from the churches in their area. One out of every six people responded that they needed some form of quality childcare during the day. This was 1969, and women were entering the workforce in huge numbers. We included those responses in the business plan we would take to the bank to ask for a bigger loan, even though the church was in default on its present loan. We got the additional money in one meeting with the bank.

2. For more on the *Imago Dei* go to http://en.wikipedia.org/wiki/Image_of_God.

# Afterword

## Now That You've Read This Book
## and Before You Begin

Bill Easum has been a cherished mentor of mine for more than ten years. In the ways that I have been blessed to be effective as a pastor, I owe so much of that to Bill. Having attempted to put Bill's coaching into practice, including this series of messages, I want to share some testimony and caution with you.

First, Bill's teaching and description of the mission of Jesus and his followers in this series of messages make my heart sing. They are, for me, a clear, biblical, and compelling vision for the church of Jesus Christ.

We who are pastors know that as important as words are, especially those words we risk to preach to our people, action and execution is just as vitally important. With that in mind, I offer the following:

Don't preach this series if you don't mean it. In other words, if you aren't ready to risk it all for this vision—your call, your position, your treasure, your life—then don't preach it. Absent of that sold-out commitment, you will inevitably blink in the face of those who oppose you. And if you preach this series, there will be those who oppose you.

Whatever you do, don't skip the important step Bill recommends in conjunction with the first message. Here's how Bill put it in San Antonio all those years ago: "I'm asking anyone who wants to join me in developing a church of thousands and transforming our city to join me at the parsonage tonight at seven o'clock, and we'll talk about it." You *must* do this. You have to strike while the iron is hot, and it will never be hotter than at this moment. If you provide for a handful of on-fire people an intimate, authentic, relational experience of joining up for the mission of Jesus, and disciple them, embolden them, and launch them, you will not lose, and you will never regret it. If you skip this crucial step, you will quickly find that your words were just that: words. Imagine how joyful and exhilarated you will feel as this group gains traction and begins to actually transform your community in the name of Jesus. And imagine how grateful you will feel when the forces of darkness attack, and this group forms around you, and protects you, and shines their increasing light. Don't skip this step. (And don't meet anywhere other than your home. Risk welcoming them fully into your life, and they will welcome you into theirs.)

Together with your group of mission activists, begin immediately to orchestrate some small but palpable wins. Find a way to go serve in your community, to be salt and light. Have someone from the group share and testify about it the following Sunday. Don't make this a sometimes thing; make it an all-the-time thing. The best kind of win you can have during this time is for new people to join you in worship. Activate this group to be a people-inviting machine. Bill Easum once told me a story about how Bil Cornelius, the founding pastor of Bay Area Fellowship, would challenge the growing group of people who launched their church. At the end of each time together, Bil would say, "If being part of this group (or church) is transforming your life, then invite ten more people to join you here next week. Why wouldn't you?"

As you follow the principles and strategies of Bill's book, you will find yourself poured out in coaching the willing and in seeking and saving the lost. You will find that you will have less time, energy, and even inclination for some of the activities that many have come to traditionally expect of a pastor. You'll get some heat. Sometimes a lot. To help lower the temperature, form and equip a care team to help you care for traditional "pastoral care" needs in the church, such as hospital and shut-in visits. Make sure the team is aware of every person who is sick or shut-in, and make sure that they visit those people. Appoint a leader of the team, and ask that person to keep you informed about the work of this team. Meet with the team twice a month to grow them and pray with them. What you are doing is making sure that the "traditional" perceived needs of your people are still cared for in an excellent way, even if not by you.

Visit Bill's website: www.churchconsultations.com. You'll find many free resources, such as articles written by Bill and others, that will help you lead strongly. You'll also find other resources, including coaching opportunities. I've found these ways to access Bill's coaching to be invaluable, and I'm certain that you will, too.

Bil Cornelius

For information on personal coaching with Bill Easum go to www.nextlevelcoachingnetwork.net.